PSYCHO-CALISTHENICS ®

A COMPLETE PROGRAM FOR PERSONAL GROWTH, SELF-IMPROVEMENT AND HAPPINESS

STEVEN WEST

McDonnell-Winchester Publishers
Distributed by
The John Day Company
New York, New York 10019

Give Light and the people will find their way.

CARL MAGEE
(slogan for Scripps-Howard Newspapers)

For information, address
McDonnell-Winchester Publishers
112 Central Park South, Suite 11F
New York City, New York 10019
(212) CI-7-7900

ISBN: 0-381-90016-9

TO JANICE—WHO TAUGHT ME TO LOVE.

TO MY PARENTS—WHO TAUGHT ME THE PRACTICAL SIDE OF LIFE.

TO HERMAN—WHO TAUGHT ME ETHICS.

TO SHELLY—WHO HELPED ME TO WRITE THIS BOOK.

Photography by Stan Patz

TABLE OF CONTENTS

1

INTRODUCTION

There is a vast amount of untapped knowledge in the world which can help you live a happier, healthier, more exciting, successful life. But only a handful of people who operate generally outside the confines of accepted society are in possession of this information.

As you read this, no fewer than 50 important human potential, mind science, and psychology groups are pioneering and expanding the horizons of human knowledge and capacity.

A group in a small Texas town is studying and perfecting the use of Alpha Brainwaves and their practical application to achieving healthier and more productive lives.

A renovated castle in a little country village in England serves as headquarters for a group working on techniques in mental health and communication skills emphasizing survival as the dominant drive in human existence.

Near the Berkeley campus, a warm, loving man sits in his wheelchair and teaches Consciousness Focusing, a method of replacing our addictions and robot-like behavior with happiness, inner peace, and tranquility.

Further south in Beverly Hills the Primal Technique began with methods designed to free people from their early painful "primal experiences" which are a major cause of neurotic behavior.

There is nothing permanent except change.

HERACLITUS

MY ROLE AND THE
ROLE OF PSYCHO- CALISTHENICS ®

An Italian psychiatrist has developed a technique called "Psychosynthesis," a new approach to release your hidden energy through a series of exercises and techniques. The Psychosynthesis theory recognizes the importance of superconscious energy.

All over the world there are groups exploring and developing new techniques. These groups share certain general characteristics. They are sincere, dedicated, and interested in the well- being of their fellow human beings.

However, these groups are often unaware of each other's work. It is as if many separate, distinct cultures were developing, coming into contact with each other only when an occasional traveler goes from one group to another.

As I traveled on my own voyage of self-discovery seeking truth, personal growth and the solutions to my problems, my role in life began to come into sharp focus. Suddenly it dawned on me that for my life to be meaningful I would have to study the different philosophies and bring together all the data, techniques, and programs developed by these groups in an innovative manner. I wanted to weld these techniques into a combined mind science which everyone could utilize to achieve their fullest potential, by drawing upon the strengths and philosophies of each of these groups.

Some of the techniques and theories I considered in evolving Psycho-Calisthenics include, in alphabetical order: Alpha Mind Control; Arica; Berne; Bio-Feedback; Body

Chemistry; Body Language; Dale Carnegie; Edgar Cayce; Consciousness Focusing; Dream Analysis; Encounter Groups; Esalen; E.S.P.; E.S.T.; Freud; Genetics; Gestalt; Napoleon Hill; Hypnosis; Jung; Irene Kassorla; Meditation; Nutrition; Parent Effectiveness Training; Para-Psychology; Positive Thinking; Primal Scream; Psychiatry; Psycho-Analytical Theory; Psycho-Cybernetics; Psychosynthesis; Silva Mind Control; Scientology; Self-Hypnosis; Trans-actional Analysis; Transpersonal Psychology; Yoga and Zen.

As I tried to find a workable format for combining these disciplines, I realized the limitations of conventional psychotherapy. These included the years of analysis required, the cost - averaging $50 per hour, and a comparatively low "cure ratio", as well as the possibility of dependence upon the analyst.

I also recognized the limitations of many of the "hip culture" movements. Often techniques and personalities in these movements ran counter to the values and opinions many of us hold. Since values and opinions may indeed be a limiting factor in accepting a discipline, many hip movements accordingly worked against their own success. No matter how liberated American society purports to be, men with flowing white robes and hair down to the middle of their backs are not prime candidates for support and sponsorship by the local PTA and the bank president. I knew my format would have to be reasonable, short-range and effective.

WHAT THIS BOOK
IS AND IS NOT

This book was written for you so that I might share with you what I consider to be the most meaningful and effective techniques for personal growth and development. This book is not a cure-all. It is merely a first step on a long, exciting journey. Neither is this book a challenge to the many human potential, mind science and psychological groups. It is rather an invitation to share, love, create, and hopefully to open up lines of communication among the diverse disciplines. We all share a common goal: to make our world a better place in which to live for all of mankind.

This book is not composed of excerpts from some academic quarterly with confusing footnotes and bibliographies. I have no ax to grind nor am I pushing any or all of the techniques.

This book was written for you, who like myself, are secretly afraid, searching for answers and tired of not knowing what questions to ask.

In general, this book is not meant for children and yet it is for children of all ages who have deep within themselves, *the child,* always fresh, alive, excited and loving.

Read and reread this book. Underline it. Write in the margins. Make it your dog-eared friend. This book outlines a 30 day starter program and you should understand each concept and idea completely before moving ahead. Remember, this book is not the end of your personal growth in Psycho-Calisthenics—it is just the beginning.

Probably the most neglected friend you have is you.

L. RON HUBBARD

The words "Mental Exercise" kept repeating itself in my mind and suddenly in a moment of special insight I realized the clear analogy between physical fitness programs and what I, in essence, was trying to formulate—a mental fitness program.

In a physical fitness program, you choose from various types of exercise (weight lifting, calisthenics, isometrics, swimming, general athletics, and so forth). You follow this program with sensible rest and diet and established goals and objectives. You set aside a certain amount of time each week for your physical fitness program, if you really want to succeed. You monitor your performance, continue and expand the exercises that work, discard what does not work, and continually substitute new exercises to enliven your routine and enhance the regimen. Initially however, the routine is established by an instructor who gives you specific exercises to perform.

To develop a mental fitness program, I chose techniques and exercises from the groups I studied. Rest, diet, and setting aside a definite time each day are important. Establishing specific goals, reviewing progress and expanding upon successful techniques are essential. The book can serve as an "instructor."

The program is called Psycho-Calisthenics. ®

2

THE BASIC EXERCISE GROUPS IN PSYCHO-CALISTHENICS

1. FUNDAMENTAL FACTS OF LIFE

In analyzing the various mind science, human potential and psychological movements, I have divided their techniques into four categories:

The fundamental facts of life are statements or concepts which give you a clear insight into your own behavior. These statements or concepts help you better understand why you behave as you do. When you study the various fundamental facts of life, you will experience a feeling known as the "Aha" reaction.

It may be after the first time you read a particular fundamental fact or the fiftieth, that an "Aha" reaction is generated. When the reality of the fact reaches into your mind and gives you a sharp insight into yourself and the world around you, it generates a resounding

"Aha, now I get it"!

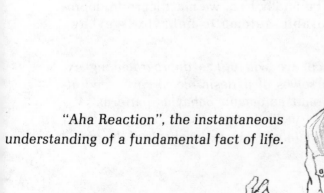

"Aha Reaction", the instantaneous understanding of a fundamental fact of life.

2. DEPROGRAMMING EXERCISES

Deprogramming exercises are techniques to help you "break" or deprogram patterns of behavior which cause you to do things you really don't want to do.

We have all developed various forms of automatic behavior. Some of this behavior is the result of attitudes and opinions we have formed during our lifetime, which make us automatically respond to particular situations.

For example, if a woman has been programmed by her parents and society that pre-marital sex is wrong, this attitude will cause feelings of guilt and reduce the pleasure of an honest, but out of wedlock sexual relationship.

Besides the automatic behavior created by inbred opinions and attitudes, we have been further programmed by painful experiences in life. If you were attacked while walking through the park on a very warm evening with a full moon shining, any time in the future when you see the moon, the park, or are out on a warm evening, you will automatically become tense and fearful. You will duplicate the behavior and emotions you felt during the attack in the park. Your subconscious mind reasons that you survived that attack and that in order to survive another incident under similar circumstances, you must duplicate the emotion and behavior you experienced during the original incident. Incidents in which our survival is threatened generate an automatic behavior pattern. If we are to be totally free, we must learn to deprogram the undesirable automatic behavior we have acquired.

To gain confidence, we will utilize deprogramming exercises to free ourselves of undesirable, programmed attitudes, opinions and automatic behavior patterns. We will experience life to its fullest, loving, sharing, trusting, laughing, completely free from the ghosts of the past.

Attitudes plus Survival Experiences create Automatic Behavior

3. MIND DEVELOPMENT EXERCISES

Mind Development exercises enhance our ability to visualize.

These are a group of techniques and exercises that you practice mentally in order to improve awareness, perception, memory, imagination, visualization, intelligence and other vital abilities.

Those exercises which help us to be more capable people are called Mind Development Exercises.

4. PROGRAMMING
   EXERCISES

Insecurity exists in the absence of knowledge.

                                    L. RON HUBBARD

Programming exercises are a way of harnessing the power of your subconscious mind to achieve your goals. Your subconscious mind is like a vast computer capable of monitoring billions of body cells and regulating hundreds of body functions.

The first step in this process is to enter the Alpha state of consciousness. The Alpha state is like a link between the subconscious and the conscious mind and you can enter the Alpha state by a simple relaxation process described in one of the first programming exercises.

It is in the Alpha state that you give instructions to your subconscious mind to help you achieve what you seek in life.

The instructions you give your subconscious mind in the alpha state are the basis for all programming exercises.

BASIC REQUIREMENTS FOR SUCCESS WITH PSYCHO-CALISTHENICS ®

Certain minimum conditions must be met to insure success in achieving a goal. The basic requirements for Psycho-Calisthenics® include:

1. THE DESIRE TO CHANGE—Psycho-Calisthenics® cannot function successfully for a person who feels forced to learn it, or is at such a low point mentally that he or she does not have the desire to change.

2. EXPECTANCY OF CHANGE—This factor of expectancy cannot be overemphasized. In short, it's really your attitude about yourself that counts. If you expect to flunk the Driver's Exam for the second time, you will. If you expect to be bored stiff visiting your old aunt, you will be. If you expect your efforts with Psycho-Calisthenics® will be successful, they will be. If you expect to be a loser, you will be. Your expectations of yourself are tremendously important.

3. NO DRUGS OR ALCOHOL—During the Psycho-Calisthenics® program it is strongly advised that you refrain from taking drugs or alcohol, both of which have an unnatural effect on your mind. (These include but are not limited to beer, wine, marijuana, heroin, cocaine, LSD, aspirin, cold tablets, and so forth).

4. PHYSICAL EXAMINATION—It is highly recommended that you undergo a complete physical examination, since there is a definite relationship between a healthy body and a healthy mind. A blood analysis test which would give you a better understanding of your blood chemistry would be helpful but is not necessary.

5. RESERVATION OF A DEFINITE TIME—Psycho-Calisthenics®, like physical calisthenics, must be practiced regularly. It is essential that you set aside a particular time of day, every day, for Psycho-Calisthenics®.

You can enter the Alpha State by a simple relaxation process.

CHAPTER

3

THE FIRST WEEK

Remember that these exercises were developed by the world's leading mind scientists and psychologists and have been organized into a clear format, with detailed day-by-day plans for you to follow.

SPECIAL INSTRUCTIONS:

1. Do not read more than is required for each day.

2. There are four exercises each day. Do not substitute. Perform the exercises exactly as they are listed.

3. In certain instances you will be asked to reread an exercise from a previous day's program. Be sure to do so and not try to redo the exercise from memory.

4. Each Fundamental Fact of Life should be read several times. Underline those words and phrases that are most significant to you. Close your eyes and reflect on the significance of each Fundamental Fact of Life as it relates to you. You should plan to spend approximately thirty minutes each day with Psycho-Calisthenics. However, the first day may require an hour or more to orient yourself.

5. On the next page there is a Psycho-Calisthenics Program Chart for the first week. It gives you an idea of your first week's activities, but, again, read and do the exercises only one day at a time.

6. Note the space at the left of the chart for date and comment. Write down anything you think is significant.

PSYCHO-CALISTHENICS® PROGRAM CHART—WEEK 1

FUNDAMENTAL FACT

DAY 1 DATE: COMMENT:..	The Moment of Now
DAY 2 DATE: COMMENT:..	The Concept of Intimacy Avoidance
DAY 3 DATE: COMMENT:..	Operating As A Cause Not An Effect
DAY 4 DATE: COMMENT:..	Taking Responsibility for your Life
DAY 5 DATE: COMMENT:..	The Concept of Insteads
DAY 6 DATE: COMMENT:..	The Web of a Belief System
DAY 7 DATE: COMMENT:..	Data Acquisition Theory

DEPROGRAMMING	MIND DEVELOPMENT	PROGRAMMING
Self Analysis	Mental Balance Sheet —Assets	Alpha Programming
Self Analysis	Mental Balance Sheet —Liabilities	Body Relaxation Method
Self Analysis	Character Analysis—Others	10 to 1 Method
Self Analysis	Character Analysis—Self	Goal 1
Letter Writing	Visualization Exercises	Goal 1, and Post Effects
The Diary	Visualization Exercises	Goal 1
Catharsis	Body Language	Goal 1

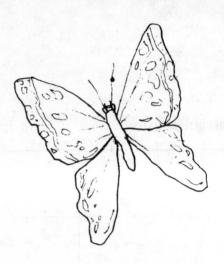

DAY 1 ● EXERCISE 1

**"THE MOMENT
OF NOW."**

FUNDAMENTAL FACT OF LIFE

Each of us must decide whether we want to live in the past, the fantasy of the future or the reality of the present, "The Moment of Now."

Many of us continually relive the past repeating the painful patterns of our childhood. Those incidents which threatened our survival or caused great personal anguish for us are constantly replayed in our minds as if they were endlessly run through a tape recorder.

Many people have tried to escape the pain of the past by attempting to live in the future. This is not to say that hoping and planning for the future is unhealthy. However, we all must live in the present. You are here—now—and life should be a celebration every day. Life must be tasted, felt and experienced. Life must be lived! Examine your own behavior and see whether you are living in the past or in the future instead of the present.

One of the main purposes in life is to derive pleasure from living. Real pleasure can only be derived from the present. You must become an observer of your own behavior.

There is only one success—to be able to spend your life in your own way.
                                    CHRISTOPHER MORLEY

You must discover which past events are constantly re-played in your mind and what fantasies of the future take up your time in the present. These are major insights into your behavior and they serve as barriers to living in "The Moment of Now."

Most people know that at times they are only partially aware. They daydream or are otherwise preoccupied. The purpose of this exercise is to heighten your feeling of reality.

The first exercise is quite simple.

A. Take a few minutes and try to make up sentences about what you are aware of at this moment. Begin with the words: "Now," or "At this moment," or "here and now." For example, "Now I am aware of a pain in the back of my neck." "At this moment I am reading this para-graph." "Here and now I am excited about the possibil-ities in my life."

If you want to develop a sense of reality the accent must be on words such as "Now" and "At this moment."

Seize the present and pin it down. Reality, however, is forever changing. A healthy feeling of reality is like the view from a car window, the scenery is always different. Although reality seems fixed and unchanging, that is not the case. Reality is as you experience it, it is your reality. You cannot experience what is so for someone else.

B. Now repeat the exercise again. Try for a few minutes to make up sentences starting with "Now" or "At this moment" or "Here and now."

Ask yourself what difficulties you encountered in this exercise. Why did you end the exercise? What were you aware of immediately preceding your termination of the exercise? Were you tired? Had you gone blank and ceased forming sentences? Or, did you perhaps quit without being aware that you were quitting?

It is important for you to answer these questions because they will give you clues to your own ability or inability to live in the "Moment of Now".

Many people attempt to read things into the instructions that do not exist. Others creatively find ways to defeat the experience. Still others intellectually perform the exercise but do not feel it. All these represent a suppression of coping with one's feelings.

The purpose of this exercise is to expand or heighten the awareness of what you were doing and how you were doing it. It will also teach you to reduce your escapes into the past and the fantasies of the future.

Do not judge any of your escapist tendencies. Simply describe them and be aware of your own behavior.

You will recapture the full feeling of reality, an experience of tremendous impact. You will feel like jumping into the air and saying, "I am walking. I am talking. I feel special. The world is really out there and I have eyes, real eyes—and ears, real ears."

If you have previously chosen to make love to an elephant and this proved to be a bruising experience, you must look at those bruises and observe the incident without self-pity and self-depreciation because the bruises of the past must not detract from "The Moment of Now."

People do not lack strength, they lack will.
                                              VICTOR HUGO

DAY 1 ● EXERCISE 2

"SELF ANALYSIS"

DEPROGRAMMING EXERCISE

Each of us has had hundreds of thousands of experiences in our lives but only a fraction of this data is readily available to our conscious mind. The purpose of self analysis is to recover individual incidents from the unconscious, bring them to the conscious level and reduce our automatic programmed behavior.

Self-Analysis is accomplished by asking yourself questions. The answers will force to consciousness individual incidents that will give you a greater understanding of your past life. Self-analysis will also bring to consciousness other related but forgotten incidents.

You may feel as though a dam has burst and a flood of insights will come to you; experiences may surface so quickly that you feel you can barely handle them all at the same time. This is completely natural since you are dealing with a part of your mind that has been largely unexplored for a long, long time.

Spend as much time as you need to with each question and get an incident fully developed in your mind. Attempt to relive that incident, to see it, smell it, touch it, hear it, feel the emotion of it, listen to it, recall your body position. Be there and re-live the experience!

BASIC INCIDENTS. This list will help you recall past experiences.

Think of a time when:

You were happy.

You built something.

You had close friends.

Somebody gave you a present.

You felt energetic.

You rode in a fast car.

Someone was looking forward to seeing you.

You saw something pleasant.

You threw away something you didn't like.

You kissed someone.

You received money.

You laughed.

You felt young.

You enjoyed life.

You played a game.

You controlled something.

You destroyed something.

You felt tranquil.

You killed a bug.

You started a machine.

You made a new friend.

DAY 1 ● EXERCISE 3

"THE MENTAL
BALANCE
SHEET"
—PART 1

MIND DEVELOPMENT EXERCISE

The mental balance sheet helps you take stock of your personal assets and liabilities. On the following page is a list of character traits. Some of these traits are more important than others. Each one is followed by three numbers indicating a value. These values will vary from one trait to another for each person.

For instance, take the trait "decisive"' If you are inclined to hesitate you should score 3 points. If you are able to decide quickly score 4 points. If you are extremely decisive score 5 points. Total your assets. The more definite the trait is for you, the more "asset" points you should give yourself. (On Day 2 you will compute your liabilities).

LIST OF ASSETS

1. Are you honest?	3	4	5
2. Are you ambitious?	3	4	5
3. Are you generous?	3	4	5
4. Are you thoughtful of others?	3	4	5
5. Do you tell the truth?	3	4	5
6. Is your attitude positive?	3	4	5
7. Are you efficient?	3	4	5
8. Are you decisive?	3	4	5
9. Are you energetic?	3	4	5
10. Are you brave?	3	4	5
11. Are you constructively and creatively aggressive?	3	4	5
12. Do you have a good sense of humor?	3	4	5
13. Are you realistic?	3	4	5
14. Are you sincere?	2	3	4
15. Are you patient?	2	3	4
16. Are you tolerant?	2	3	4

17. Can you concentrate well?	2	3	4
18. Are you punctual?	2	3	4
19. Do you have good health?	3	4	5
20. Is your appearance fair, good, handsome (beautiful)?	3	4	5
21. Is your general build fair, good, excellent?	3	4	5
22. Are you well-coordinated and skillful?	3	4	5
23. Do you have good vision?	3	4	5
24. Are you intelligent?	3	4	5
25. Have you established goals?	3	4	5
26. Are you talented?	3	4	5
27. Do you have a good job?	3	4	5
28. Are your finances good?	3	4	5
29. Do you have a good female/ male relationship?	3	4	5
30. Are you respected by your friends?	3	4	5
31. Are you well liked?	3	4	5
32. Are you athletic?	3	4	5

Your Asset Total = _____

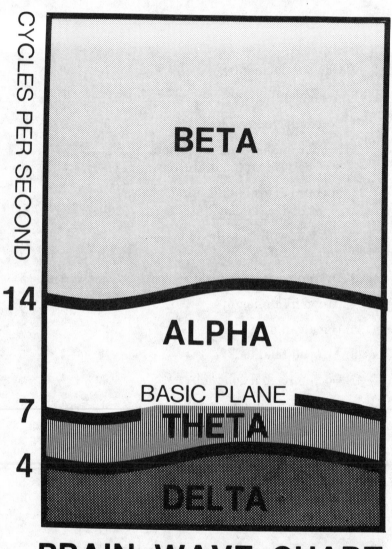

BRAIN WAVE CHART
LEVELS OF CONSCIOUSNESS

DAY 1 • EXERCISE 4

"ALPHA DIMENSION"

PROGRAMMING

The Alpha Dimension is simply a relaxed state of mind. In scientific terms the brainwave frequency is between 7 and 14 cycles per second in the alpha dimension. In ordinary living the brainwave frequency is generally between 14 and 22 cycles per second. This is known as the Beta dimension.

By learning to enter the alpha dimension, you can have direct access to your subconscious mind and can direct it in a way that will help you achieve your goals and objectives. The entire alpha technique is designed to achieve systematic relaxation which is the key to the alpha state. The instructions may seem lengthy, but with a little practice you will be able to enter the alpha dimension in a few minutes. While in the alpha dimension you can give instructions to your subconscious.

A) PREPARATION FOR ENTERING THE ALPHA DIMENSION

1. Before entering the alpha state of consciousness, you must create a safe place for yourself; a place safe from interruption or any possibility of physical discomfort.

2. Before entering the alpha dimension, remove your shoes and loosen any tight clothing so that there is no constriction of your body. (Ladies, off with those bras)!

3. You may find it more comfortable to lie on the bed or the floor or to sit with your feet propped up. If you find yourself drifting off to sleep, move to a comfortable chair.

4. Keep your body in an open position. Do not cross your legs or arms. Keep your hands open.

5. Repeat to yourself the fact that you know with total certainty that you are capable of entering the alpha dimension.

6. Believe and expect that the instructions you give your subconscious mind will be converted into tangible reality.

7. The instructions you give your subconscious mind must be clear and concise — not contradictory.

8. Begin your programming with simple objectives and goals. You will not find it purposeful to start off by programming that you become the President or Mickey Mouse.

9. When you get feedback and a few successful results, go on to your next goal even before the written instructions tell you to program a new goal.

10. Read the instructions on how to exit from the Alpha dimension before entering the Alpha dimension.

How to enter the Alpha Dimension
by the 5 to 1 method
from the book Psycho-Calisthenics®
by Steven West

33 1/3 RPM

PLACE COIN HERE IF SOUNDSHEET SLIPS

Psychology Industries, Inc.,
112 Central Park South,
Suite 11F,
New York, N. Y. 10019

MFD. IN U.S.A. BY 818751X DEERFIELD, ILL.
EVATONE
SOUNDSHEETS

Please note that a flexible record has been bound inside the back cover of this book. This record may be listened to in order to assist you in entering the alpha dimension. Detach it carefully and listen to the record three times prior to actually using the record to enter the alpha dimension.

B) ENTERING THE ALPHA DIMENSION

1. Close your eyes and take two or three very deep breaths. Hold each breath for a count of four, then exhale. While exhaling you may sigh, moan, whatever; just let it all out.

2. With your eyes closed take a deep breath and while exhaling, visualize and silently repeat to yourself the number 5—5 times. If you expel the air before visualizing and saying the number, it is not important. Just resume your normal breathing pattern. Remain quiet and breathe naturally several times.

3. With your eyes closed take another deep breath and while exhaling, visualize and silently repeat to yourself the number 4—four times. It does not matter whether your numbers come through sharp or muddled, in sections or parts, on a chalk board, popping out of the rumble seat of a 1930 Ford as long as you sense that they are there. It is the effort that counts. Remain quiet, breathe naturally several times. R-E-L-A-X.

4. With your eyes closed, take another deep breath and while exhaling, visualize and silently repeat to yourself the number 3—three times. Remain quiet and breathe naturally several times. R-E-L-A-X.

5. Take another deep breath, still with your eyes closed, and while exhaling, visualize and silently repeat to yourself the number 2 three times. Remain quiet and breathe naturally several times. R-E-L-A-X.

6. Take another deep breath, still with your eyes closed, and while exhaling visualize and silently repeat to yourself the number 1 three times. Remain quiet and breathe naturally several times. R-E-L-A-X.

7. Now tell yourself silently that you have reached a new level of quiet, a healthier, relaxing inner consciousness, the Alpha Dimension. For the next two or three minutes, just completely R-E-L-A-X.

C) HOW TO LEAVE THE ALPHA DIMENSION

This first day, two or three minutes of light Alpha relaxation will be enough to give you a taste of the Alpha Dimension. When programming is to be done, it should be done just before leaving the Alpha dimension. Remember to begin with simple goals.

To Exit From The Alpha Dimension, tell yourself that you will count from 1 to 5 and that at the count of 5 you will open your eyes, feel perfectly wonderful, free from all tension, healthier, completely relaxed and feeling better than ever.

Proceed to count slowly 1, 2 and then 3. Pause for just a moment after the count of three and repeat to yourself silently that at the count of 5 you will open your eyes.

Now count slowly 4 and 5, then at the count of 5 and with your eyes opened, silently tell yourself,"I am wide awake, alert, free from all tensions, completely relaxed, healthier and feeling better than ever."

DAY 2 ● EXERCISE 1

"THE CONCEPT
OF INTIMACY
AVOIDANCE"

FUNDAMENTAL FACT OF LIFE

Quite often the basic drive to love and the basic drive to survive find themselves in conflict. If you are thirty years old, you have spent 15,778,800 minutes on this planet. There is a strong probability that in those minutes you have had many negative experiences in your relationships with people.

It could have been the nurse who was a bit rough in handling you at birth. Maybe it was your mother who failed to change your diapers with sufficient care. It could have been a playmate who took your pet turtle or a little girl in the third grade who told you you were ugly. Maybe it was a seventh grade science teacher who flunked you, or the coach of the football team who told you you were too skinny to play. Maybe it was the professor in college who made fun of you in front of the class. Possibly it was the first time you were fired, or rejected by a lover. But all these events and scores like them need not be very traumatic in order to leave an indelible and painful mark. You become conditioned to avoid close relationships with people.

Every time your nurse, mother, teacher, good friend, coach, professor, employer or lover rejects you, it reinforces a self-imposed pattern which says—in order to survive, you must avoid intimacy with people, and guard your innermost feelings and defend them from others.

You choose superficial, safe relationships. Your desire to survive has surpassed your desire to love. You now live in the twilight zone between love and safety, neither feeling love nor being truly safe. This effort to avoid intimacy affects a great deal of your behavior. A complete understanding of intimacy avoidance and how it relates to you will give you a better understanding of why you are unable to share your thoughts and love with others.

You will begin to realize that the experiences you had thirty years ago in a crib, ten years ago in a classroom, or two weeks ago in a lover's bed, should have no significance in your present life and that you must live in the present.

Living a lonely life is only satisfactory to a worm whose principal social and sexual objective in life is copulating with himself.

No matter how bad past experiences might have been, you have to go on living—so you may as well do everything you can to make it the best possible life you can have. If you got food poisoning once from something you ate, you can't give up eating. If you bought a suit or a dress that you realized was unbecoming, you don't give up buying clothes forever unless you run away to a nudist colony. The same is true of other unpleasant experiences. If you had a bad business venture or a bad love affair you don't give up working or loving unless you go on welfare or take a vow of abstinence, neither one of which is really an alternative. When your alarm goes off tomorrow morning, come out loving!

*I beg of you to remember that wherever our life touches yours we help or hin-der... wherever your life touches ours, you make us stronger or weaker...
There is no escape—man drags man down, or man lifts man up.*

BOOKER T. WASHINGTON

DAY 2 ● EXERCISE 2

DEPROGRAMMING

"SELF ANALYSIS"

TIME ORIENTATION. This list will help you go back to the periods in your life in which you acquired automatic programming. You will learn to go back and forth on your own time track.

Recall an incident:

1. That occurred far in the past.

(a) what year was it? (b) the month? (c) the hour?

2. That occurred yesterday.

(a) what was the hour? (b) what was the date?

3. That occurred in the recent past.

(a) what kind of clothes were people wearing?

(b) what were you wearing?

4. When you felt energetic.

(a) when was it? (b) what did you do?

5. That occurred last New Year's Day.

(a) time of day?

6. Your 13th birthday.

(a) what did the furniture in your house look like?

(b) who was with you on your birthday?

(a) the year? (b) the season?

7. The last birthday party you attended.

(a) the season? (b) the year?

8. Your last special date with someone.

(a) where did you go? (b) what time did you go out?

9. The last animal you played with.

(a) how old were you? (b) how big was the animal?

DAY 2 ● EXERCISE 3

"THE MENTAL BALANCE SHEET" —PART 2

MIND DEVELOPMENT

Evaluate your liabilities the same way you assessed your assets in the previous day's exercise.

If you are never depressed, score 3 points. If you are depressed sometimes, score 4 points. If you are always depressed, score 5 points. If you are never anxious, score 3 points. If you are sometimes anxious, score 4 points. If you are always anxious, score 5 points.

When you are through, total the score for your liabilities. The assets minus the liabilities will give you your mental balance sheet.

LIST OF LIABILITIES

1. Are you dishonest?	3	4	5
2. Are you inefficient?	3	4	5
3. Are you cruel?	3	4	5
4. Are you self-centered?	3	4	5
5. Are you depressed?	3	4	5
6. Do you have a negative attitude?	3	4	5
7. Are you anxious?	3	4	5
8. Do you feel guilty?	3	4	5
9. Do you feel inferior?	3	4	5
10. Do you avoid responsibility?	3	4	5
11. Are you indecisive in public?	3	4	5
12. Are you lazy?	2	3	4
13. Are you selfish?	2	3	4
14. Are you irritable?	2	3	4
15. Are you indifferent?	2	3	4
16. Are you critical of others?	2	3	4
17. Do you think you are more important than others?	2	3	4
18. Do you have difficulty concentrating?	2	3	4
19. Are you a perfectionist?	2	3	4

20. Are you too passive?	2	3	4
21. Do you have bad health?	3	4	5
22. Is your appearance unattractive?	3	4	5
23. Is your build poor?	3	4	5
24. Are you awkward?	3	4	5
25. Do you have a poor education?	3	4	5
26. Do you have a negative female/ male relationship?	3	4	5
27. Are you disliked?	3	4	5
28. Do you have a bad memory?	3	4	5
29. Are you dissatisfied with your job?	3	4	5

Your Liability Total   =   _____

If your Balance Sheet (Assets minus liabilities) score is:	Your General Mental Condition:
− 25 or less	Extremely poor
− 15 to − 24	Poor
− 5 to − 14	Below Average
− 4 to + 5	Average
+ 6 to + 15	Above Average
+ 16 to + 25	Very Good
Over + 25	Excellent

DAY 2 ● EXERCISE 4

"BODY RELAXATION METHOD"

PROGRAMMING

On the first day you read the instructions for entering the Alpha dimension and entered a preliminary alpha level using the 5 to 1 method. You also learned how to come out of the Alpha dimension. (Reread all instructions from Day 1, Exercise 4).

Today you are going to enter the Alpha dimension again but this time you are going on to a deeper state of concentration. You will deepen your entry into the Alpha dimension by using the body relaxation method, which is described below. By deepening the Alpha level you will be more directly in touch with your subconscious.

Keeping your eyes closed you are going to relax every part of your body systematically. Eventually you will be able to enter the Alpha state with your eyes open. Remember, first enter the Alpha dimension by the 5 to 1 method, then continue.

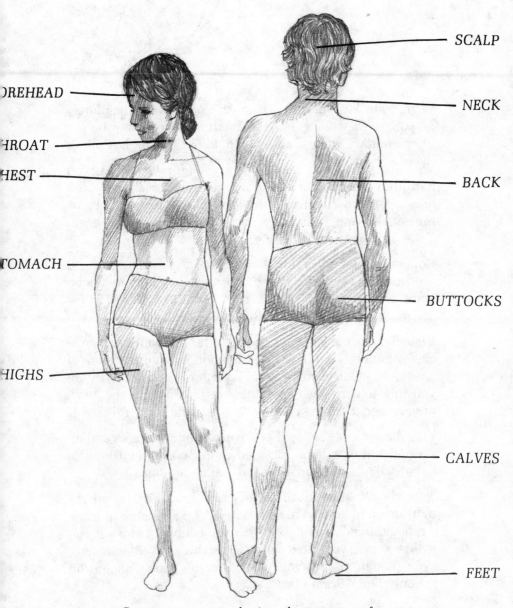

SCALP

NECK

BACK

BUTTOCKS

CALVES

FEET

OREHEAD

HROAT

HEST

TOMACH

HIGHS

Concentrate on relaxing these areas of
your body in your Body Relaxation Exercises.

With your eyes closed, visualize your scalp completely relaxing with all the tension floating away. Now take a deep breath. Exhale. Pause and hold for 5 seconds. Relax.

Visualize all the tension leaving your forehead as if you had little valves attached to it. Pretend that as you mentally open those valves, orange liquid representing the tension leaving your body, comes out of your forehead. Take a deep breath. Exhale.

Concentrate on your throat and relax all the tensions and pressures in that area. Put this part of your body in a deep state of relaxation. Take a deep breath. Exhale. Pause and hold for five seconds. Relax.

Visualize the back of your neck and feel all your neck muscles completely relax with all tension leaving the back of your neck. This is going to be a very relaxing and very rewarding experience. Feel the tension leaving the back of your neck. Take a deep breath. Exhale.

Visualize your chest as if you were opening valves and all the tension was being drained out. Take a deep breath. Exhale. Pause and hold for five seconds. Relax.

Now visualize the muscles on your back and feel all the tightness and tension disappearing. You are going to enter a relaxed, healthful state of consciousness. Later on you will feel as if you have had a refreshing three-hour nap, even though at first you will be in the Alpha dimension for only 5 or 10 minutes.

Visualize the muscles in your stomach totally relaxing. Imagine each muscle is another valve being opened and that all the tightness and tension is disappearing. Take a deep breath. Now exhale. Pause and hold for five seconds. Relax.

Visualize your buttocks with all the tension leaving. Imagine you are floating on a cloud, totally relaxed. Take a deep breath. Exhale.

Visualize your thighs with all the tension leaving. Imagine that balloons are attached to your thighs and that you are floating in a beautiful blue sky. Take a deep breath. Exhale. Pause and hold for five seconds. Relax.

Visualize your calves with all the tension and tiredness leaving them. Take a deep breath. Exhale.

Visualize the bottom of your feet with all the tension leaving them. Imagine you have wings attached to your feet and that you are floating over a blue-green ocean. Take a deep breath. Exhale. Pause and hold for five seconds. Relax.

Now you have become more relaxed and you are ready to enter a deeper state of consciousness.

After approximately five minutes exit the Alpha dimension by counting from 1 to 5 as described in Day 1, Exercise 4.

Wise men are instructed by reason; men of less understanding, by experience; the most ignorant, by necessity; the beasts by nature.

MARCUS TULLIUS CICERO

DAY 3 • EXERCISE 1

"OPERATING AS A CAUSE NOT AN EFFECT"

FUNDAMENTAL FACT OF LIFE

At some point in your life you must decide whether you want to be pushed around or a person who can stand on his own two feet. You must decide whether you will be buffeted by a constant parade of stimuli, each pushing your emotional buttons at random or whether you will command your own destiny and control your personal pleasure.

Most of us go through life like leaves in the wind, drifting aimlessly, eventually settling down, drying up, and decaying.

To achieve personal growth and pleasure, you must exercise control over events in your life rather than being controlled by the environment.

On an elemental level, this may mean sending back a cold cup of soup, even if you think it may embarrass the waiter, yourself, or just be an awkward experience. It means that you must choose your own clothing, your own school, your own apartment, your own car, your own food and friends.

On a more sophisticated level, it means you must control your own destiny to achieve the work, love, success, and happiness you seek in life. You must not be dominated by past experiences which trigger outdated, inappropriate responses and rob you of happiness.

This does not mean that you should manipulate others to selfishly achieve your own objectives. It means that in a loving, warm way you can motivate others to help you achieve your goals by offering them reasons to share your goals. You should communicate your needs and goals to others and invite them to share their goals with you and thus combine efforts to achieve mutual success.

You can control your environment, the temperature, the light, the moisture, the visual and audio stimulus. You can cause the events you desire to happen.

Look at all the events in your life in which you simply reacted to other people's stimuli. Look, too, at those things in your life which you always thought were beyond your control.

Look at all those events and recapture the "personal space" you have abdicated to others. Take control of your life, bit by bit, and begin to operate as a positive force not as a helpless victim.

Shake free of your present way of thinking. If someone comes at you with a baseball bat you wouldn't just stand there waiting to get hit over the head, you would defend yourself. But you can learn to think farther than that, to talk and carry yourself with confidence so that people will think twice before attempting to victimize you. You will like the things you do better because you will know you really chose to do them. You will like yourself better because you will feel you have control over your life. You will like other people better because you won't feel you're being manipulated by them.

DAY 3 ● EXERCISE 2

"SELF ANALYSIS"

DEPROGRAMMING EXERCISE

COMPARING INCIDENTS. This list will help you recover your ability to make comparisons that cover long time spans.

Compare your clothing today with the clothing you wore when you were 6 years old.

Compare your hairdo now with the one you had when you were 15 years old.

Compare the condition of something you have now to the condition it was in when you originally bought it.

Compare something which is big now to what it was like when it was smaller.

Compare something which is old now to what it was like when it was young.

Compare the way the sun shines in the morning with the way it shines in the afternoon.

Compare winter and summer.

Compare a long time and a short time.

Compare something when it is hot to that same thing when it is cold.

Compare the light when it is bright and when it is dim.

DAY 3 • EXERCISE 3

"CHARACTER ANALYSIS"

MIND DEVELOPMENT EXERCISE

Divide a large sheet of paper in half. On the left side list the positive personality traits and on the right side the negative personality traits listed below. Next to each of the traits, write the name of the person who you think, most typifies that trait in terms of attitudes, emotions, and behavior.

POSITIVE	NEGATIVE
Tolerant	Intolerant
Accept their own mistakes	Blames others
Self-starter	Has to be coaxed or driven
Finds good in others	Gossips maliciously
Punctual	Always late
Open-minded	Opinionated
Polite	Boorish and brutal
Listen and talks intelligently	Talks, but does not listen
Alert and to the point	Vague and illogical
Cooperates with others	Dominates others
Dependable	Shirks responsibility

POSITIVE	NEGATIVE
Self-reliant	Timid and fearful
Shows courage	Buckles under pressure
Shows consideration	Inconsiderate or abuses others
Flexible	Inflexible
Kind and appreciative	Discourteous to subordinates
Organized	Disorganized
Enjoys children	Dislikes young people
Affectionate	Cold
Accepts criticism	Loses temper easily and blames others
Humorous, able to laugh at self	Lacks sense of humor
Reasonable	Unreasonable
Patient	Impatient, easily frustrated
Open and honest	Secretive or deceptive
Unpretentious	Ostentatious
Happy	Glum
Optimistic	Pessimistic
Healthy and uncomplaining	Chronically ill

POSITIVE	NEGATIVE
Creative	Narrow-minded
Fair and just	Plays politics, shows favoritism
Relaxed	Tense
Forgiving	Vengeful
Intelligent	Dull

By applying these traits to people you know, you will be a better judge of the personality of others. It will help you decide whom you should associate with to achieve your goals in life.

DAY 3 ● EXERCISE 4

THE 10 TO 1
METHOD

PROGRAMMING

On Day 2 you entered the Alpha dimension by the 5 to 1 method and you deepened your entry into the Alpha dimension by the body relaxation method. Today you will enter a deeper state of the Alpha dimension by using the 10 to 1 method.

You will:

(1) Enter the Alpha dimension by the 5 to 1 method.

(2) Deepen the Alpha dimension by the body relaxation method.

(3) Further deepen the Alpha dimension by the 10 to 1 method.

As you visualize each number in your mind and count backward, with each succeeding number you will enter a deeper state of the Alpha dimension.

Visualize the number 10 in your mind. Relax your body completely. Take a deep breath. Now exhale. Visualize the number 9 in your mind. Take a deep breath. Now exhale.

Continue until you have reached number 1. You have now deepened your entry into the Alpha dimension and are in direct touch with your automatic subconscious mind and are prepared to achieve your goals and objectives in life.

After entering the Alpha dimension and deepening that state by using the above methods, come out of the Alpha dimension by the 1 to 5 method. (Be sure to reread all instructions).

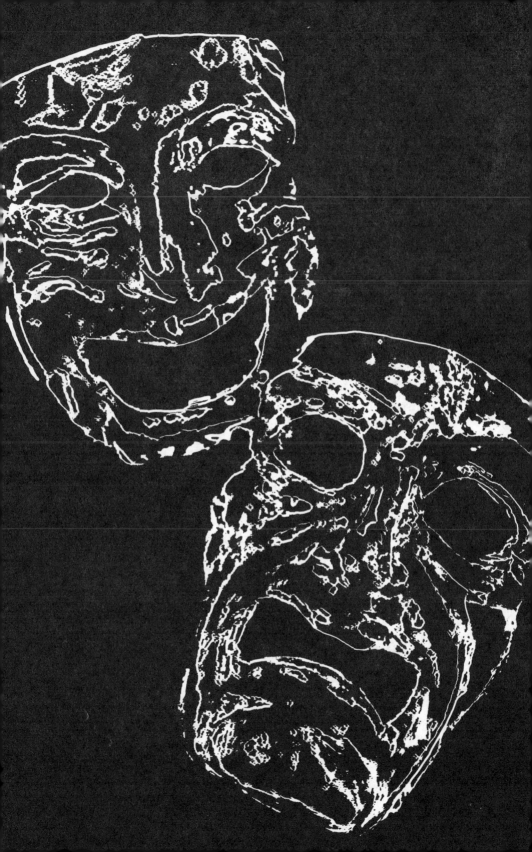

DAY 4 • EXERCISE 1

"TAKING RESPONSIBILITY FOR YOUR LIFE"

FUNDAMENTAL FACT OF LIFE

Each of us has spent a great deal of time dwelling in the past and blaming others for our problems and failures. If you are willing to live in the present and are eager to operate as a positive cause in your life, then you must take the responsibility for all your experiences.

You create your own reality. Right now you have the ability to control your environment and cause the favorable effects you seek.

You have the power to exert your own will in life, to take down artificial barriers that separate you from favorable consequences. You can choose the role of Romeo or rodent, swinger or schlepper.

If you have failed in a business venture, it is easy not to take the responsibility and say — "If only the bank had given me additional money. If only my partner had not been so lazy. If only the stores had purchased more of my product." But in fact, since you do operate at will in life, then it was you who selected the bank and partner and products to sell to the stores. And, if you did not select the bank, partner and products to sell, at least you acquiesced in someone else's decision.

If you were employed by a company whose bank withdrew its support, or owners or partners were unethical, or whose products were not of the highest quality, then it was your choice to either join that company or not join that company. You are responsible for every decision, every outcome. If you are deceived by someone, if your health is poor; if you didn't like the movie you saw, these negative results are all a function of the decisions you have exercised or abdicated.

You could have chosen a more loving companion by learning more about that person. You also could have chosen a better diet and a better regimen that would promote better health.

You could have acquired more data about the movie you did not like, questioned friends, read reviews, and in general made a more informed decision about whether the film was in keeping with your taste.

In the game of life you have unlimited potential and ability, and an unending number of daily decisions, with many possible results. The more you develop your abilities to their fullest, carefully pursuing your decisions, gathering all the data you can and using it to the best advantage, the more the result, which is the combination of ability and decision-making, will be favorable.

Once you take responsibility for your life, your self-pity will begin to disappear.

You will be more capable of loving and more loved yourself because you will no longer blame someone else for your unhappiness. You will actively seek data to make more meaningful and effective decisions. You will say, "I will not be an effect, I will be a cause." You will insist on living in the present and refuse to dwell on past unhappiness.

Intimacy avoidance will also become a thing of the past. You will realize that no one can do anything to you that you don't want them to do and therefore you will not fear being in love and being intimate with anyone. Take responsibility for your life—celebrate life and love!

Those of us who have looked to others to make our decisions, must remember with sadness that the lady who told us which fork to eat with and what to say and do, Amy Vanderbilt, committed suicide. The lady who told us how to solve our marital difficulties, Anne Landers, recently announced her plan to divorce.

The mind is an iceberg—it floats with only one-seventh of its bulk above water.

SIGMUND FREUD

DAY 4 ● EXERCISE 2

**"SELF
ANALYSIS"**

DEPROGRAMMING

This list will help you develop your visual recall and depth perception.

Can you remember seeing something which was:

Very bright.	Pretty.
Dark.	Mysterious.
Vast.	Lazy.
Moving.	Warm.
Flat.	Cheerful.
Deep.	Lovable.
Colorful.	Passionate.
Slow.	Blurred.
Pleasant.	

DAY 4 • EXERCISE 3

"CHARACTER
ANALYSIS"

MENTAL DEVELOPMENT

After placing the name of a person who most typifies each of those traits listed under Mental Development Exercise on Day 3 (Exercise 3), decide which traits best relate to you. After you have completed the exercise note how many positive and negative traits apply to you. This is your own personality balance sheet. By applying these traits to yourself, you will be able to see your strengths and weaknesses and take action to develop your personality to its fullest potential.

DAY 4 ● EXERCISE 4

Goal I

PROGRAMMING

Let's tune into the following telephone conversation:

Voice: Good morning. This is World-Wide Directions Inc. May I help you?

You: Yes. I'd like some direction.

Voice: Most certainly, Sir, where are you planning to go?

You: Well . . . uh . . . mm . . . oh, some very nice place.

Voice: Sorry, Sir, I didn't hear you. Where to?

You: Well, it's important that I get to some very nice place. I don't want to waste a great deal of time. I really want to get to some very nice place.

Voice: I don't understand. Some very nice place like . . . where?

You: Oh, some very nice place where I can be successful, be happy. Where I can have a good income, get a new car, maybe be my own boss or be an executive with a big company. Some very nice place where I can be more relaxed, have some peace of mind and maybe do right by my wife and kids, where things are great for the whole family. Just give me the route, I'll pay for it with cash.

Voice: But, sir, I can't give you directions until you can tell me EXACTLY WHERE YOU WANT TO GO!

Psycho-Calisthenics® will enable you to discover many things about that dynamic, powerful, wonderful human being that is you. Incredible as it may sound, Psycho-Calisthenics® is the vehicle through which you may achieve every goal and objective you desire. This very moment may be the most critical moment of your life.

Right here and right now it is of utmost importance that you answer the vital question: "What do I want?" It is not enough to talk in general terms about happiness or success. You must sit down and make a complete list of your goals and objectives. Put them in the simplest, practical and exacting terms.

Make three lists: (1) The Things I Need Now (2) Things I Like to Dream About Having and (3) The Personal, Human Qualities I Need and Desire.

Imagine that you have just won a contest, the prize being a blank check to take care of everything you need right now. The following are some suggestions but write your own list:

(1) The Things I Need Now:

house furnishings

car fixed

bills paid

income/insurance

new dress

dental work

rent/mortgage

improved health

color television

new washing machine

Now, let's go on to the next list. These are not needs, but things you want, wild things, shoot for the sky things, for now or in the future:

Things do not change; we change.

THOREAU

DAY 4 EXERCISE 4 (con't.)

(2) Things I Like to Dream About Having:

Mercedes-Benz

$200,000 house

75-foot yacht

an original masterpiece

year-long trip around the world

$500,000 bank account

two oil wells

Possession is at best, only one small phase of happiness and success. We need certain qualities of personality and character for continued happiness and success. Now list the personal, human qualities you need and desire:

(3) Personal, Human Qualities I Need And Desire:

better use of time

greater intimacy in my personal relations

to be healthier

to complete tasks I start

greater ability to concentrate

ability to generate enthusiasm

more creative thought

a sense of profound self-respect

You now have lists of those tangible and intangibles which make up your desires. To turn those lists into concrete goals you must use them as check lists to achieve your goals consistent with your life and your personality.

First examine each list carefully and be sure it is as complete as you can make it. Then check each item against the following:

1. Is it something I really want?

(or is it just to impress someone or something for "kicks?")

2. Is there any contradiction in my goals?

(If you want a $150,000 house with an $18,000 yearly income, then you have to change your salary or income goal)

3. Is it a positive rather than a negative goal?

(Is it something you want to have rather than something you want to get rid of?)

4. Is the goal totally and concisely expressed?

(Not a new, well-made sports car or a hot, flashy import but, rather a showroom-new, red Porsche, Targa Model with [list in detail everything you want on it as though you had already paid for it in cash].)

5. Is it realistic?

(Briefly, if it's a goal someone might attain, it's realistic)

6. Have I set the goal high enough?

(This is important. Goals can be self-limiting. Check your self-image. Be certain to set your goals high enough to effect meaningful change in your life. Don't worry about how to achieve these goals. That's the job of Psycho-Calisthenics®.

PROGRAMMING DIRECTIONS   —Goal I

On Day 3 in Exercise 4 you entered the Alpha dimension by the 5 to 1, body relaxation method and the 10 to 1 method. Today you will program positive goals based on your newly developed goal list. First you will work on goals from list (1) Things I Need Now and list (3) The Personal, Human Qualities I Need and Want.

Before entering the Alpha dimension, read all of List I. Choose the first goal you want to achieve.

Then use the 5 to 1, body relaxation, and 10 to 1 method to enter the Alpha dimension.   Programming goals will take approximately 10-20 minutes. After programming your goal, leave the Alpha dimension by the 1 to 5 method.

PROGRAMMING ALL POSITIVE RESULTS—Goal 1

1. Enter the 5 to 1 and the 10 to 1 level of the Alpha dimension.

2. Visualize in your mind's eye the successful achievement of your goal. Repeat at least six times the fact that you have achieved that goal. For example, if you want $10,000 immediately hold the image of the $10,000 in your mind. Stay relaxed and focus on the image. If the image is not clear, it doesn't matter, just sense it to be there.

3. Mentally say to yourself, "I have $10,000. I see it, I feel it, I can experience it. The $10,000 is mine." Keep repeating a positive statement about possession of the money.

4. Now creatively expand the visualization, i.e. Visualize yourself at a bank endorsing a check for $10,000. See the face of the check made out to you with the exact amount written in. See yourself handing it to the teller who gives you ten one thousand dollar bills. Visualize yourself hold-

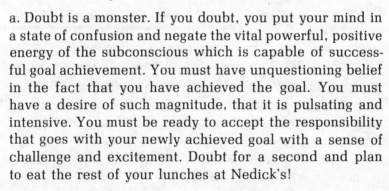

ing the money. Feel it, sense it, know that it is there. Continue to repeat mentally: I have $10,000. I see it, I feel it, I can experience it. The $10,000 is mine to use for any purpose.

5. Examine each bill individually and arrange them so that you may see each laid out. At the same time repeat positive statements of possession. Stay relaxed! You may imagine choosing to take the $10,000 in cash to the bank and deposit it in your checking account and then proceed to write checks, repeating all the while the verifications of possession.

6. Programming your goals from Lists 1 and 3 initially may run from 10 to 20 minutes, but may be expanded in the future.

7. *The following is of MAJOR IMPORTANCE:*

a. Doubt is a monster. If you doubt, you put your mind in a state of confusion and negate the vital powerful, positive energy of the subconscious which is capable of successful goal achievement. You must have unquestioning belief in the fact that you have achieved the goal. You must have a desire of such magnitude, that it is pulsating and intensive. You must be ready to accept the responsibility that goes with your newly achieved goal with a sense of challenge and excitement. Doubt for a second and plan to eat the rest of your lunches at Nedick's!

b. Once you have completed your programming and left the Alpha dimension, forget completely and let the programming of your inner consciousness do the job. There are two exceptions.

c. In the morning, in your waking state of outer consciousness, read aloud to yourself *ALL* of the goals from your three lists. Do the same thing in the evening before retiring. This is a vital part of your programming effort because it will keep open the proper channels for success.

DAY 5 ● EXERCISE 1

"THE CONCEPT OF INSTEADS"

FUNDAMENTAL FACT OF LIFE

When purposes and goals are not achieved in life, we find substitutes to dull the full impact of failures and therefore we are not forced to confront life as it really is. These substitutes have been called "insteads."

When we were small and got angry, our parents stopped us immediately just as their parents stopped them. Our anger scared them because they were inexperienced in dealing with their own feelings of anger. Since we were unable to deal with anger or failed purposes in general, we agreed to "insteads."

Overeating is commonly used instead of anger, as is alcoholism and gambling. Your wife may be unhappy because you went to play tennis instead of staying home and playing with your child. But in fact if you did not get some relaxation on the tennis courts you feel you would have just exploded. Your wife may be furious that you did not spend time with your child. You are hurt because she does not understand your needs. Instead of telling her what your needs are, you squelch your anger and run to the refrigerator and stuff food into your mouth.

Boredom is also an "instead." People who are unable to say they are angry and that they have failed to achieve a particular goal say they are bored. Boredom has become very fashionable and is permitted by your mommy and society. Boredom is really the squelching of your feelings in order not to experience them.

Depression is also an "instead" for anger or a failed purpose. Depression is merely a lower level than boredom.

Criticism is also an "instead" for anger. Criticism is a way of not feeling your own unhappiness and failure by finding fault with someone else.

Physical illness is another common "instead." An endless parade of colds, colitis, skin and back problems, flu and fatigue are often a diversionary effort on the part of your subconscious mind when you have failed to achieve a goal. Your subconscious mind has come to the illogical conclusion that in order to survive you cannot feel and experience anger and that one way to survive is to divert your attention to a physical ailment. Therefore there will be no time in your conscious attention span to deal with the real problems in your life.

This kind of behavior is often compounded by a form of learned helplessness in which you were rewarded for being an invalid as a child.

Another "instead" is constant diversion. Many people use the continual noise of a television set or a radio, endless telephone calls, or keep their nose in a book, all instead of thinking about their problems. As a matter of fact, some people may just sit and read this book instead of actually practicing Psycho-Calisthenics® and really changing their life.

Take a look at the "insteads" in your life and see how they prevent you from living in the present and from reaching your goals.

Opinion has caused more trouble on this little earth than plagues or earthquakes.

VOLTAIRE

DAY 5 • EXERCISE 2
LETTER WRITING

DEPROGRAMMING

Letter writing is an effective technique to communicate with people who have been involved in painful or survival related experiences with you.

Simply stated, write that person a letter and tell him exactly the way you feel. Tell him about your love. Tell him about your pain. Tell him about the experiences you shared together and what they meant to you. Get all the feelings and suppressed desires on the piece of paper.

The letter can be long or short. Go back and correct it or leave it the way it is. You can mail it, file it, or tear it up. But if you choose to mail it, remember that if the feelings you express are in opposition to the feelings of the person you were writing to, you may experience a break in affinity or communication with that person.

DAY 5 • EXERCISE 3
"VISUALIZATION EXERCISES"

MENTAL DEVELOPMENT

The purpose of these visualization exercises is to develop your ability to make a mental picture of the things you want to achieve in life and to develop the ability to focus your mental energy so that you can achieve your goals. The more vividly you can create a mental picture, the more likely that, in combination with your other Psycho

Calisthenics® exercises, you will be able to achieve your goals in life.

Close your eyes and enter the Alpha dimension by the 5 to 1 method, the body relaxation method, and 10 to 1 method.

1. Visualize a white background. On that white background mentally draw:

a. A square.

b. A circle.

c. A triangle.

d. A rectangle.

2. Now color in each of the four geometric figures with the following colors:

a. Red square, circle, triangle, rectangle.

b. Blue square, circle, triangle, rectangle.

c. Green square, circle, triangle, rectangle.

d. Yellow square, circle, triangle, rectangle.

3. Draw the following:

a. Three squares with the second square twice the size of the first square and the third square twice the size of the second square.

b. Repeat the exercise using circles.

c. Repeat the exercise using triangles.

d. Repeat the exercise using rectangles.

DAY 5 ● EXERCISE 4

POST EFFECTS

PROGRAMMING

During Day 4 you entered the Alpha dimension by the 5 to 1 method, the body relaxation method and the 10 to 1 method. Then you began to program your first goal.

Today, in addition to entering the Alpha dimension by the above methods and programming your final goal for 10 minutes, you will use the post-Alpha instructions to help you get additional benefits from Alpha programming.

After using the post Alpha instructions come out of the Alpha dimension by the 1 to 5 method.

POST ALPHA INSTRUCTIONS

Before coming out of the Alpha dimension, repeat some post-Alpha instructions to yourself that will help you achieve your objectives:

1. Every time I function in the Alpha dimension, I will receive positive benefits, both physically and mentally.

2. I can use the Alpha dimension to help myself both physically and mentally.

3. I can help my loved ones both physically and mentally when I use the Alpha dimension.

4. I can use the Alpha dimension to help anyone who needs help.

5. I will always use the Alpha dimension in a constructive and positive manner.

6. If I ever attempt to hurt anyone while I am in the Alpha dimension, I will not be able to function at this level.

DAY 6 ● EXERCISE 1

"THE WEB OF
A BELIEF
SYSTEM"

FUNDAMENTAL FACT OF LIFE

Each of us has, during the course of our lifetime, evolved hundreds of opinions and beliefs about life that we feel to be true. Many of us believe that capitalism is the best economic system or that monogamy is the best social arrangement. All of us have certain ideas about what Christianity really means or how to raise children.

If someone asked you your opinion on a subject, more often than not, you would have a pat answer, one that you give unthinkingly by now. You might be asked what you think about sex education in the school system? Without conscious re-examination of your thoughts you might respond, "That is a wonderful thing, children should learn more about sex," or "Sex should be taught at home and is a very private matter."

Every decision you make is dictated by ideas and beliefs you have held for most of your life.

You have ceased to live in the present. Therefore, your unchanging attitudes serve to defend you from fully experiencing the present. These unchanging attitudes allow you to keep a distance from reality and thus avoid risking rejection.

Many people feel their belief systems are necessary for survival and that they defend them from potentially negative experiences. Such an attitude is based on the erroneous assumption that the world and reality are static states and therefore our beliefs can be unchanging too. In fact, our attitudes are actually estimates of reality and each of us perceives a "reality" differently.

You must begin to ask yourself what attitudes and beliefs act as a shield against the outside world and isolate you from real experiences. You must question every belief you have and repeat this process throughout your lifetime. Attitudes that you presently hold may be relatively valid today, but in the light of new experiences, your beliefs and theories may cease to be realistic.

A re-evaluation of your belief system is very much like a monthly physical inventory in a manufacturing plant. If you engage in a reasonable amount of interaction with others, those beliefs will change just like the inventory in a factory.

Examine your beliefs and study the stereotypes you hold in your mind. Develop your ability to judge each person on an individual basis.

Are your beliefs really arbitrary barriers that stand between your personal growth and pleasure? Do your feelings about money limit you in terms of your enjoyment of finances or in making the best use of your money? To function in the present you must experience life as it exists in the present. You must abolish a belief system which is based on the past. Because Psycho-Calisthenics® is going to help you change your life, try to think of yourself as starting life with a clean slate. Forget the past. You have probably been wearing the same hairstyle, the same kind of clothes, the same perfume, drinking the same cocktail, watching the same television program for years. You certainly don't have to change any of that but think about it. Just because you have always done something a certain way doesn't mean you are sentenced to a life term of continuing the same habits.

DAY 6 ● EXERCISE 2

DEPROGRAMMING

THE DIARY

One way of desensitizing a new, painful experience is by keeping a diary. By writing in your diary, you give yourself an opportunity to desensitize painful experiences by reviewing them on a conscious basis. In addition, by recapturing your experiences in general from your subconsciousness, you begin to control a greater portion of your data bank.

By reflecting on the day's activities you have an opportunity to rechart your course for the next day in order to better achieve your purpose. Try keeping a diary for a week.

DAY 6 ● EXERCISE 3

"VISUALIZATION EXERCISES"

MENTAL DEVELOPMENT

Now visualize the following sights:

1. A home.

2. A car.

3. An airplane.

4. A television set.

5. A refrigerator.

6. A tree.

7. A bookcase.

8. A sink.

9. A chair.

10. A typewriter.

Color each of those objects red, blue, green and yellow in your mind. Next take each of the objects and create a second one of the same kind, twice the size of the first and a third one twice the size of the second. Then visualize the first three objects (home, car, airplane) all together. Visualize the next three objects (television, refrigerator, tree) all together. Now visualize the next four objects (bookcase, sink, chair, typewriter) all together.

Visualize the following objects in motion:

1. A train.
2. An airplane.
3. A car.
4. A boat.
5. Piano keys.
6. A bicycle.

Next imagine a classroom with a blackboard. Visualize the number 5 in the middle of the blackboard. It is written with chalk, fairly large and well defined. Keep the number 5 steadily in your consciousness. Then to the right of the number 5 visualize the number 2.

Now you have two figures, a 5 and a 2, making 52. Dwell for a while on the number 52 and after a while imagine the appearance of the number 4 at the right of the 2. Now you have three figures written in white chalk, 5-2-4, making the number 524. Visualize this number for a while. Continue adding numbers until you are unable to remember the sequence.

Here is another visualization exercise. Study a photograph for one minute. Then close your eyes and evoke the image you have just seen and describe it completely to yourself. This exercise will help you measure your ability to visualize things. With further exercises the number of details you can accurately record will increase and the length of time needed to gain a vivid mental image will decrease. Visualization exercises will help you develop your imagination and your ability to program success.

DAY 6 ● EXERCISE 4

PROGRAMMING
GOAL 1

Enter the Alpha dimension by the 5 to 1 method, the body relaxation method and the 10 to 1 method. Then program your first goal.

Today, in addition to programming your first goal for ten minutes and entering the Alpha dimension by the above methods, you will use the post-Alpha instructions to help you get additional benefits from Alpha programming.

After using the post-Alpha instructions come out of the Alpha dimension by the 1 to 5 method.

POST — ALPHA INSTRUCTIONS

Before coming out of the Alpha dimension, repeat some post-alpha instructions to yourself that will help you achieve your objectives:

1. Every time I function in the Alpha dimension, I will receive positive benefits, both physically and mentally.

2. I can use the Alpha dimension to help myself both physically and mentally.

3. I can help my loved ones both physically and mentally when I use the Alpha dimension.

4. I can use the Alpha dimension to help anyone who needs help.

5. I will always use the Alpha dimension in a constructive and positive manner.

6. If I ever attempt to hurt anyone while I am in the Alpha dimension, I will not be able to function at this level.

DAY 7 • EXERCISE 1

FUNDAMENTAL FACT OF LIFE   "DATA ACQUISITION THEORY"

Most problems in life are caused by having an insufficient amount of data to develop an appropriate solution. In each problem you should ask yourself, "What data am I missing? What data must I acquire so I can logically compute an appropriate solution?"

For instance, you may be wondering whether a certain young lady or man is in love with you. You can spend long, restless hours pondering on the possibility on whether true love exists. Your mental computer will burn up excess energy attempting to find the solution. The Data Acquisition Theory tells you, however, that in order to find the solution to this problem, you must obtain additional data.

You can read psychological studies on love to better understand what goes on in a loved one's mind. You can try to understand the way in which a person acts when in love and relate this personality profile to the personality profile of your potential loved one.

You can discreetly ask mutual friends if your would-be loved one has indicated any inclinations as they relate to love and you. Or you can flat out ask the loved one, "How do you feel about me? Do you love me as much as I love you?"

Instead of burning up mental midnight oil operating with limited information, you should aggressively seek out additional information. Nearly every successful business or marriage is not just good luck but a lot of hard work that mainly consists of learning all about a business or a person, constantly pursuing information and applying it to the goal at hand.

Getting more data for your goal is like a jigsaw puzzle where you get your solution by reaching out for the additional pieces and putting them in the right place.

Sometimes a statistic is needed. For example, you may be sitting there unhappily pondering a tremendous stack of bills. You keep saying, "Oh my God! How am I going to be able to pay these bills? These bills are past due, my credit will be ruined."

The acquisition of data theory as it relates to statistics will say, "Instead of moping around worrying about how you're going to pay the bills, you follow a logical course."

1. Add up all the bills and place them in a logical sequence; when they are due, by week or month.

2. Analyze all of your assets to determine your ability to pay the bills.

3. Compute your income and how it can help toward paying the bills.

4. Consider the possibility of obtaining additional time to pay the bills.

5. Determine the exact amount and availability of funds which can be used to pay your bills.

6. Determine how many additional sources of revenue not presently available to you can be used toward paying your bills.

7. Now build a logical plan to pay your bills.

8. Make a budget that will avoid a similar problem in the future.

If you have a problem that is bothering you right now, take steps to acquire the necessary data and the problem will begin to resolve itself and eventually disappear. Then you can fully experience the present without worries.

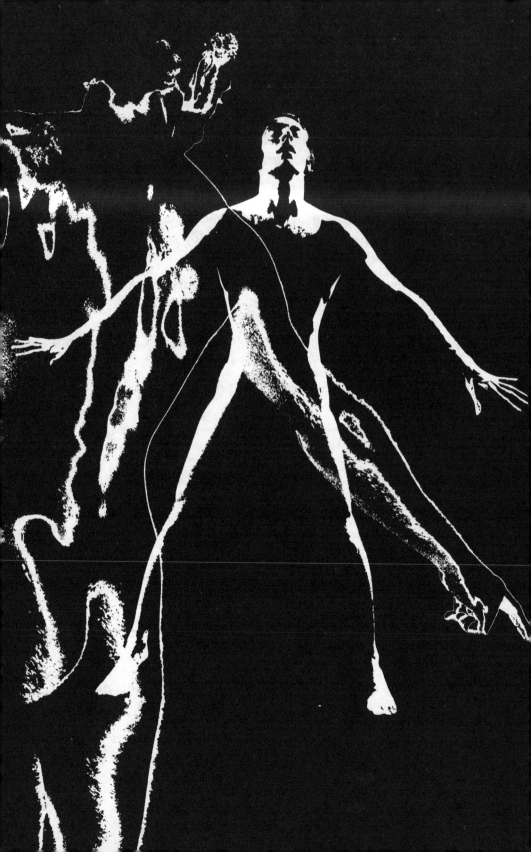

DAY 7 ● EXERCISE 2

DEPROGRAMMING

CATHARSIS

Many schools of psychology are based on the idea of your talking to a sympathetic listener who does little more than say "Aha" and repeat what you have just told him. The Catharsis technique of speaking on any subject you so desire is an effective one. Just decide without a great deal of thought what you wish to talk about, or start talking with no advanced decision. If you can, use a tape recorder.

This form of random audio diary will help you reach thoughts that have been buried below the conscious level and also help you compose scattered thoughts that are at your conscious level.

Ask yourself certain questions after each exercise in catharsis:

1. Why did I choose this subject to talk about now?

2. What insights have I gained about myself by listening to what I had to say?

3. What problems have I defined for myself whose solution would better assist me in achieving my purpose?

4. What previous incidents in my life caused me to feel the way I felt when I did the catharsis exercise?

5. What steps am I going to take to solve the problems that were revealed in the catharsis exercise.

| Dejected | Awed | Defensive | Coy | Sceptical |

DAY 7 • EXERCISE 3

MIND DEVELOPMENT

"BODY LANGUAGE ANALYSIS"

We all tend to repeat the behavior, gestures, and attitudes we acquired in our early survival experiences when similar experiences occur now.

A clue to understanding yourself and to understanding others is body language. Body Language is made up of gestures, the positions of your body and the general way you carry yourself and express yourself. These gestures and expressions are learned very early in life as reactions to childhood experiences. Body Language is direct communication from your subconscious mind.

Our gestures must be viewed as a whole since an isolated gesture can be misleading. However, if one sees clenched fists, we know they are generally associated with tension and anger. Folded arms can be generally associated with aggression and defensive behavior. A slow, plodding walk is often associated with failure and rejection. Finger tapping is often a sign of anxiety or a decision that has just been made. You can observe the facial expressions of people and learn to associate fearful, happy, pensive, and puzzled looks with particular behavioral patterns.

These gestures and movements are signals from your subconscious mind and can help you understand your own subconscious and the attitudes of others. Analyze 10 different forms of your own body language. Try to associate your feelings with body language position.

| Bored | Calculating | Seductive | Confident | Thoughtful |

DAY 7 • EXERCISE 4

PROGRAMMING   GOAL 1

Enter the Alpha dimension by the 5 to 1 method, the body relaxation method and the 10 to 1 method. Then program your first goal.

Today, in addition to programming your first goal for ten minutes and entering the Alpha dimension by the above methods, you will use the post-Alpha instructions to help you get additional benefits from Alpha programming.

After using the post-Alpha instructions, come out of the Alpha dimension by the 1 to 5 method.

POST ALPHA INSTRUCTIONS

Before coming out of the Alpha dimension, repeat some post-alpha instructions to yourself that will help you achieve your objectives:

1. Every time I function in the Alpha dimension, I will receive positive benefits, both physically and mentally.

2. I can use the Alpha dimension to help myself both physically and mentally.

3. I can help my loved ones both physically and mentally when I use the Alpha dimension.

4. I can use the Alpha dimension to help anyone who needs help.

CHAPTER

4

THE SECOND WEEK

SPECIAL INSTRUCTIONS

1. Do not read more than what is required for each day.

2. Each day there are four exercises. Do not substitute. Perform the exercises just as they are listed.

3. Do not be lazy and try to redo the exercise from memory. If you are not sure of an exercise, go back and reread it.

4. Each Fundamental Fact of Life should be read three times. Then close your eyes and reflect upon its significance as it relates to you. In total, you will spend approximately 30 minutes each day with your Psycho-Calisthenics® program.

5. On the next page is a Psycho-Calisthenics® Program Chart for the second week. But be sure to read the exercises and do them one day at a time.

6. Note the space at the left of the chart for the date and comment. Write down anything you think is significant.

PSYCHO-CALISTHENICS ® PROGRAM CHART—WEEK 2

FUNDAMENTAL FACT

DAY 8 DATE: COMMENT:..	The Concept of the ARC Triangle
DAY 9 DATE: COMMENT:..	The Doctrine of Confrontation
DAY 10 DATE: COMMENT:..	The Concept of Change
DAY 11 DATE: COMMENT:..	Agreement and Support
DAY 12 DATE: COMMENT:..	Control and Protest
DAY 13 DATE: COMMENT:..	The Concept of Specialized Knowledge
DAY 14 DATE: COMMENT:..	How to Understand People

DEPROGRAMMING	MIND DEVELOPMENT	PROGRAMMING
Self Analysis	The Exercise of Forgiving	Goal 1
Self Analysis	Disinhibition Exercise	Goal 1
Self Analysis	Compulsions	Goal 1
Self Analysis	Exercise of Sexual Arousal	Goal 1
Visual Projective Technique	Ethics Audit	Goal 1
Modern Meditation	Psychic Energy Release	Goal 1
Other Meditative Techniques	Psychic Energy Release	Goal 1

. . . that which one fears, one becomes.

DAY 8 ● EXERCISE 1

THE CONCEPT
OF THE ARC
TRIANGLE

FUNDAMENTAL FACT OF LIFE

The three concepts of affinity, reality, and communication are very much interrelated. Affinity may be defined as an attractive force between people, a sympathy marked by community of interest.

Reality may be defined as a true state of affairs.

Communication may be defined as the act of passing along information or feelings.

By taking the first letter of Affinity, Reality and Communication, one can represent this as an ARC triangle.

The more you increase your affinity for another person the more you share reality with that person. When your affinity or liking for a person increases you will automatically communicate better with that person.

Similarly when the reality you share with another person is increased, you will find that you increase your affinity or liking of that person. You will also find that when you and someone else increase your mutual beliefs about reality, you will automatically find yourself in better communication.

To the extent one of the sides of the ARC triangle is increased, the other two sides will be increased. Also, to the extent that affinity, reality or communication is decreased, then the other two triangle sides will be decreased.

If you want to get closer to another person, then you have to communicate with that person and when you communicate with him you will find that you and he will like each other more.

Communication is not an attack on someone. Communication is sharing your feelings. It is having someone actually receive the message that you are sending. Communication is not a chance to protest what some one has been doing to you, because you must take responsibility for your own life. It is you who has been "doing it" to you. Communication does not mean having a temper tantrum like a two-year old child. Communication is sharing. It is by definition a two-way channel; receiving and sending. For communication to work, you must be a good listener, as well as a good talker.

It has been said that to truly know a man you must walk a mile in his shoes. All of us have known people who we thought we had figured out and then when we knew them better we found that the mental image we had of these persons was wrong.

Don't assume that you can tell everything about someone by looking at him. People who look wealthy may be wearing their last good suit, people sitting at the opera may wish they were at a ball game, while the janitor in your office building may wish he could afford to go to the opera. If you make an effort to get below the surface with people you will always be rewarded. Be open with people, look forward to communicating with them and they in turn will be eager to listen to you.

The more you share in common with another person, the more you will love that person and be able to live with him. The more you love a person the more you uncritically accept that person for what they are. The more you give people freedom to be themselves, the better your communication and understanding of others will be.

Understanding the relationship between affinity, reality, and communication is essential in helping you live life to its fullest and achieving your goals.

There is one thing stronger than all the armies in the world: and that is an idea whose time has come.

VICTOR HUGO

DAY 8 ● EXERCISE 2

"SELF ANALYSIS"

DEPROGRAMMING

This list will help you develop your recollections of taste experiences. Reflect on each item.

Remember when you tasted:

Soup.	Fish.
Eggs.	Steak.
Bread.	Cheese.
Coffee.	Potatoes.
Tea.	A cocktail.
Milk.	Ice cream.
Cereal.	Fruit.
Dumplings.	Something raw.

Your favorite dish.

Something special in a fine restaurant.

Something you ate outdoors.

Something you ate when you were very hungry.

Something you had never eaten before.

DAY 8 ● EXERCISE 3

"THE EXERCISE
OF FORGIVING"

MIND DEVELOPMENT

Make a list of all the people who have hurt you. Whatever you think these people may have done to you, you must realize that you always had the option to act rather than be passive when you were hurt. Therefore you must take responsibility for your hurt and dismiss from your conscious and subconscious mind the blame or hate you have for others. Hate and unhappiness only serve to keep you from living up to your full potential.

Enter the Alpha dimension by the 5 to 1 method, the body relaxation method, and 10 to 1 method. Then systematically review the list of people you want to forgive and spend several minutes on each person deciding how to tell them that you forgive them. If your list is long you may complete this exercise after the 30 day program. The experience of forgiving is an important exercise.

As you work on your Psycho-Calisthenics® exercises you may actually want to contact these people and tell them how you feel. Don't expect that they will all be happy to hear from you but do try to contact them.

DAY 8 ● EXERCISE 4

GOAL 1

PROGRAMMING

Enter the Alpha dimension by the 5 to 1 method, the body relaxation method and the 10 to 1 method to program your first goals.

In addition to entering the Alpha dimension by the above methods and programming your first goal for 10 minutes, use the post-Alpha instructions to gain additional benefits from Alpha programming. (You may program a second goal from your Human Qualities or Desires list if you prefer.)

After using the post-Alpha instructions, come out of the Alpha dimension by the 1 to 5 method.

DAY 9 • EXERCISE 1

"THE DOCTRINE OF CONFRONTATION"

FUNDAMENTAL FACT OF LIFE

The Doctrine of Confrontation means that the things you won't face dominate you and the ones you confront you control.

We all have unpleasant experiences and in order to survive we have a natural tendency to avoid conflict and stay away from negative experiences. An ostrich sticks his head in the sand and hopes by so doing he will avoid conflict. If you have ever seen an ostrich with his head in the sand you will have noticed a rear end perfect for kicking.

Later, you will make a list of all the problems facing you and begin to take positive action to solve these problems. You will experience tremendous relief when you take the first step in facing your problems. The sooner you confront a situation, the more control you have over its outcome.

You must observe your behavior and notice when you are avoiding a problem. You must reprogram yourself to take positive action instead of avoiding the problem. As you confront your problems you will be taking responsibility for your own life, controlling your environment, and living more successfully.

DAY 9 • EXERCISE 2

"SELF ANALYSIS"

DEPROGRAMMING

This list will help you develop your ability to recall experiences with your sense of touch.

Can you recall an incident when you touched:

Another person.	A doll.
Your hair.	Silk.
A child.	Velvet.
Something comfortable.	Your body.
Something pretty.	A strong person.
A generous hand.	Water.
A pleasant letter.	Something warm.
An object you loved.	Something cold.

Something which gave you confidence.

Something which delighted you.

A telephone when you received good news.

A cool bed on a warm night.

Something this morning.

Freedom in general may be defined as the absence of obstacles to the realization of desires.

BERTRAND RUSSELL

DAY 9 • EXERCISE 3

"DISINHIBITION EXERCISE"

MENTAL DEVELOPMENT

In order to achieve your goals and really live in the present, you must learn to confront the things that trouble you. Inhibition keeps you from achieving something you want. You can free yourself to reach your goals if you try.

The following is a list of things that may be preventing you from really enjoying life. This is a very personal exercise. *Make a list of at least 20 things that you feel inhibited about, and as long as they are not illegal or harmful, you should attempt to do them.*

Are you afraid to:

Speak to a stranger.

Speak in front of a group.

Have a complete sexual relationship.

Eat with your fingers in a restaurant.

Buy something which is completely frivolous.

Tell a rude person that he is a son of a bitch.

Wear a revealing bathing suit.

Send a friend flowers (that applies to ladies sending flowers to men also).

Scream at the top of your lungs wherever you are now.

Buy an article of clothing you have always wanted, but were too embarrassed to purchase.

Introduce yourself to a person you have always wanted to meet.

Buy something for your home that you always wanted to have.

Rent a limousine for an hour.

Run up to a friend of yours and give him or her a big kiss.

Tell the person you love the most in the world how you really feel about him or her.

DAY 9 ● EXERCISE 4

GOAL 1

PROGRAMMING

Enter the Alpha dimension by the 5 to 1 method, the body relaxation method and the 10 to 1 method. Program your first goal.

In addition to entering the Alpha dimension by the above methods and programming your first goal for 10 minutes, use the post-Alpha instructions to gain additional benefits from Alpha programming.

After using the post-Alpha instructions, come out of the Alpha dimension by the 1 to 5 method.

DAY 10 ● EXERCISE 1

"THE CONCEPT OF CHANGE"

FUNDAMENTAL FACT OF LIFE

You must examine your life and decide which behavior patterns need changing and which you want to keep. Try to repeat this exercise often.

Change is vital in achieving your goals and objectives. The more willing you are to change, the more you will be fulfilled as a person. Examine your own behavior and the behavior of others. The less you change the less you will control your own life.

Change may be as simple as deciding if the soap your mother always used is still really the best soap for you. Or it may be as complex as deciding to move to a climate or environment which is more pleasing to you.

A professor, when asked about his final exams, said that the questions are the same every year; however, the answers always change.

Take a good look at your life and wherever you see that you are stuck in a rut there is an underlying cause that you need to examine.

DAY 10 ● EXERCISE 2

"SELF ANALYSIS"

DEPROGRAMMING

This list will help you develop your recollection of emotions.

Can you recall an incident when:

Someone was angry.

You wanted something.

You were happy.

You felt affectionate.

You were amused.

You liked something.

You were surprised by something pleasant.

You finished something successfully.

You were attached to something.

You blushed.

You were energetic.

You were satisfied.

You cared for someone.

You were confident.

You influenced someone.

You laughed.

You were in love.

You were passionate.

You were happy you hurt someone.

You woke up to a beautiful day.

DAY 10 • EXERCISE 3

"COMPULSIONS"

MIND DEVELOPMENT

Compulsions are a constant pattern in your life which make you repeat a certain kind of behavior whenever a familiar situation occurs. A compulsion forces you to behave in a particular way even when you don't consciously want to.

Compulsions are the result of highly charged survival incidents that you encountered as a child and which dominate your subconscious mind. These experiences keep you in pain, and prevent you from fully experiencing life and love.

Such compulsions are an attempt to divert your mind from painful experiences.

Someone who jogs three miles a day compulsively knows they can concentrate on jogging instead of facing a problem that bothers him. A constant nail biter has learned to acquire gratification on an elementary level to replace the emotional support he could not get as a child. A compulsive urinator has learned to discharge emotional pressure instead of dealing with it.

The nymphomaniac has learned to use physical stimulation to hide emotional inadequacy. An alcoholic has learned to dull his senses so he will not experience the feelings of unhappiness that constantly plague him.

Compulsions begin with a survival-related incident in which you developed a way of avoiding pain. Compulsions may also be caused by a mistaken idea that in order to achieve a particular emotional outcome, one must repeat a particular experience.

Examine the compulsions in your life. Try to reason out what incidents may have caused your compulsion. Use your Psycho-Calisthenics® exercises to gain further insight into yourself and your compulsions. You must overcome those early experiences which caused the compulsions by using deprogramming techniques.

Are you compulsive about:

Talking.

Drinking.

Sexual relations.

Pacing.

Fidgeting.

Eating.

Wearing certain clothes.

Getting hurt in a relationship.

Smoking.

Jogging.

Looking in the mirror.

Spending too much money.

Combing your hair all the time.

Cooking.

Cheating.

Flirting.

Hand washing.

Running away.

Masturbating.

Sleeping.

Bathing.

Neatness.

Being on time.

Nail biting.

Fighting.

Staring.

Lying.

Gambling.

DAY 10 ● EXERCISE 4

GOAL 1

PROGRAMMING

Enter the Alpha dimension by the 5 to 1 method, the body relaxation method and the 10 to 1 method. Program your first goal.

In addition to entering the Alpha dimension by the above methods and programming your first goal for 10 minutes, use the post-Alpha instructions to gain additional benefits from Alpha programming.

After using the post-Alpha instructions, come out of the Alpha dimension by the 1 to 5 method.

DAY 11 ● EXERCISE 1

"AGREEMENT & SUPPORT"

FUNDAMENTAL FACT OF LIFE

The natural drive to love makes all of us seek to increase our affinity with others. Therefore, we all seek ways to find agreement with others. This drive to obtain agreement is related to the love drive.

Agreement or support may be as simple as the approving glance of your boyfriend when he picks you up or as complex as being elected President of the United States. Agreement is a vote of confidence.

The more you agree with someone, the more affinity you feel for that person and the better able you are to communicate with him. When you are unhappy, you do not have agreement with someone and the reverse happens.

Be aware of your own behavior and observe how you attempt to achieve harmony with others. The more that you can honestly achieve agreement with others, the more you can achieve your goals in life. Observe the behavior of others. Notice their behavior as they seek agreement and support and try to understand their motives.

DAY 11 • EXERCISE 2

"SELF ANALYSIS"

DEPROGRAMMING

Can you remember when:

You conquered something.

You surprised somebody.

You found you were anxious for no reason.

You discovered your suspicions were unfounded.

You got rid of something that was bothering you.

You were happy.

Someone understood you.

You stopped someone from crying.

You felt free.

You helped someone.

You felt young.

You won a game.

You were glad to be with someone else.

You received a present you liked.

You made something.

You made someone obey you.

You realized it was the last day of school.

DAY 11 • EXERCISE 3

"EXERCISE OF SEXUAL AROUSAL"

MIND DEVELOPMENT

Lie on your bed naked with your hands at your sides, but not touching your body. Now, through whatever mental pictures you choose, begin to reach a state of sexual excitement.

For men, the purpose of this exercise is to achieve an erection without touching yourself, strictly through mental stimulation. For women, the purpose of this exercise is to achieve vaginal lubrication and nipple erection through mental stimulation. The purpose of this exercise is to help you control your body through mental processes rather than physical manipulation.

DAY 11 ● EXERCISE 4

GOAL 1

PROGRAMMING

Enter the Alpha dimension by the 5 to 1 method, the body relaxation method and the 10 to 1 method. Program your first goal.

In addition to entering the Alpha dimension by the above methods and programming your first goal for 10 minutes, use the post-Alpha instructions to gain additional benefits from Alpha programming.

After using the post-Alpha instructions, come out of the Alpha dimension by the 1 to 5 method.

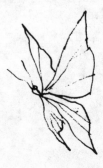

DAY 12 ● EXERCISE 1

"CONTROL AND PROTEST"

FUNDAMENTAL FACT OF LIFE

We all function best when we are free from conflict. All our lives we have been conditioned to believe that certain things are so. We have been told that it is important to live in a big home in the country. We have been told that marriage is a must for young adults. We have heard over and over again about the Protestant Ethic and the importance of work. We have all developed a belief system which controls us and makes for automatic unthinking behavior.

Take the little boy who is repeatedly told by his father about the importance of money and at age seven is mowing lawns, at 14 delivering packages, at 21 selling encyclopedias and at 28 building a business empire all because he is mercilessly driven by forces beyond his control.

Wanting to succeed is admirable. Being compelled to succeed because others have told us to is not. When we discover we do not need 16 million dollars to achieve happiness and purpose in life, we are freed from the control others have over us.

Suddenly the business dynamo sits on the beach thinking about the world around him and decides not to work anymore. He decides to achieve the tranquility he has missed. The business dynamo is going through a control and protest pattern in which:

1. Control is established through old attitudes and beliefs.

2. Control is enforced by people around us who impose their opinions and expectations on us.

3. Realization occurs that such people are no longer in a position to dictate our behavior.

4. We begin to behave in a different manner according to our own desires.

We often go overboard in the other direction in an attempt to achieve by excess what we missed by limiting our actions. Observing control and protest in your life and in the lives of others is a vital tool in understanding yourself.

DAY 12 ● EXERCISE 2

"VISUAL
PROJECTIVE
TECHNIQUE"

DEPROGRAMMING

Think of any person with whom you would like to talk, living or dead, whether known to your or not, and mentally put that person in a chair facing you.

With your eyes closed or open, talk to that person and imagine each of his or her responses.

It can be your mother in the chair. Tell her how you feel. Tell her the things you always wanted to say but could not because you were either unable to communicate with her or afraid to communicate with her. Imagine her responses, visualize her sitting in the chair opposite you. Don't be afraid to become emotional or cry (the more, the better). All this means is that you are coming in contact with some buried experiences which need to be relived and desensitized. When this happens you will better be able to live in "The Moment of Now."

You may choose a relative, a friend, a person you would like to meet or even an enemy for this technique. Imagine each of their responses and talk with them just as if they were in the room with you.

DAY 12 ● EXERCISE 3

"ETHICS AUDIT"

MIND DEVELOPMENT

Ask yourself each of the following questions, which concern your ethics and integrity. Think about the answers and decide how you acted in the past, why you acted as you did, what effect these reactions have had in your life and the image you hold of yourself today.

You may want to take action to repair unethical breaches and help anyone you have damaged by your behavior.

Have you ever:

1. Cheated on an examination?

2. Cheated on your income tax?

3. Lied about your age?

4. Lied about your marital status?

5. Had sexual relations with a married person other than your own wife or husband?

6. Committed a crime?

7. Ignored a traffic ticket?

8. Padded an expense account?

9. Ignored an error in a bill?

10. Spied or eavesdropped on someone?

11. Deliberately opened another person's mail?

12. Intentionally injured someone?

13. Committed an act of vandalism?

DAY 12 EXERCISE 3 (con't.)

14. Intentionally injured or killed an animal?

15. Bullied or abused someone?

16. Gotten someone fired or demoted because you did not like them?

17. Taken a kickback?

18. Spread a malicious rumor?

19. Harrassed someone?

20. Enjoyed someone's misfortune?

21. Refused to help someone in distress?

22. Wished someone were dead so that you could have their money and possessions.

23. Cheated while playing a game?

24. Misrepresented yourself to a prospective employer?

25. Stood-up a date?

Ask yourself what other unethical things have you done. Don't waste time condemning yourself for the unethical actions of the past but, instead, take immediate action to prevent yourself from repeating these actions in the future.

DAY 12 • EXERCISE 4

GOAL 1
PROGRAMMING

Enter the Alpha dimension by the 5 to 1 method, the body relaxation method and the 10 to 1 method. Program your first goal.

In addition to entering the Alpha dimension by the above methods and programming your first goal for 10 minutes, use the post-Alpha instructions to gain additional benefits from Alpha programming.

After using the post-Alpha instructions, come out of the Alpha dimension by the 1 to 5 method.

DAY 13 ● EXERCISE 1

"THE CONCEPT OF SPECIALIZED KNOWLEDGE"

FUNDAMENTAL FACT OF LIFE

Society has now reached a point where you cannot have material success without specific knowledge. Specialization is the way of life in advanced industrial societies. We have one doctor who looks at our noses and another who looks at our sex organs.

A copywriter recently applied at an advertising agency for a job handling a dog food account and proudly told the interviewer that he had had two years of experience with a dog food manufacturer. The interviewer flabbergasted the copywriter by asking him if he had worked on a *wet* or *dry* dog food account.

If a homemaker is to succeed on a limited budget, she must acquire specialized knowledge of the marketplace. She must learn which stores offer the best bargains in which categories on which days. She must compute the amount of money she may save versus the cost of transportation to acquire the specials. She must become an amateur economist, computing the cost of electricity for a freezer, the capital depreciation of the freezer, potential repairs on the freezer, the future value of money and relate this to the cost savings on purchasing a side of beef.

If a homemaker develops these traits she will achieve an important purpose in her life; her personal pleasure at having more money to spend. Such a person has taken responsibility for her life and by doing so operates in the present and does not have to think of how it might have been if she had more income.

A successful homemaker has learned the principle of data acquisition. In her own way she has been as successful as a businessman or doctor who practices his profession after years and years of training.

For a businessman to be truly successful he must try to know as much law as his attorney and as much accounting as his accountant. A good businessman is a salesman, a financier, a manufacturer, an industrial psychologist, an inventor, a lover and a negotiator. The more specialized knowledge he acquires, the more power he has.

If you want to succeed, you must acquire specialized knowledge to achieve your goals.

DAY 13 ● EXERCISE 2

"MODERN MEDITATION"

DEPROGRAMMING

Meditation has been a successful tool used by millions of people. It is helpful to use the Alpha dimension entry techniques in conjunction with basic forms of meditation.

Enter the Alpha dimension through the 5 to 1 method, the body relaxation method, and the 10 to 1 method. Now say to yourself, "I am going to empty my mind of all thoughts while I count to 3 and when I count to 3, I will observe those thoughts which come to my mind. I will detach myself from those thoughts and merely be present to them on a nonjudgmental basis, 1-2-3."

Examine the thoughts which surface. Look at them, carefully note the people and places, examine the colors and shapes. Notice everything but remain detached from the experience.

After meditating re-examine your thoughts on an evaluative basis: (1) What pictures surfaced? (2) Why did they surface? (3) What significance do these thoughts have to you right now?

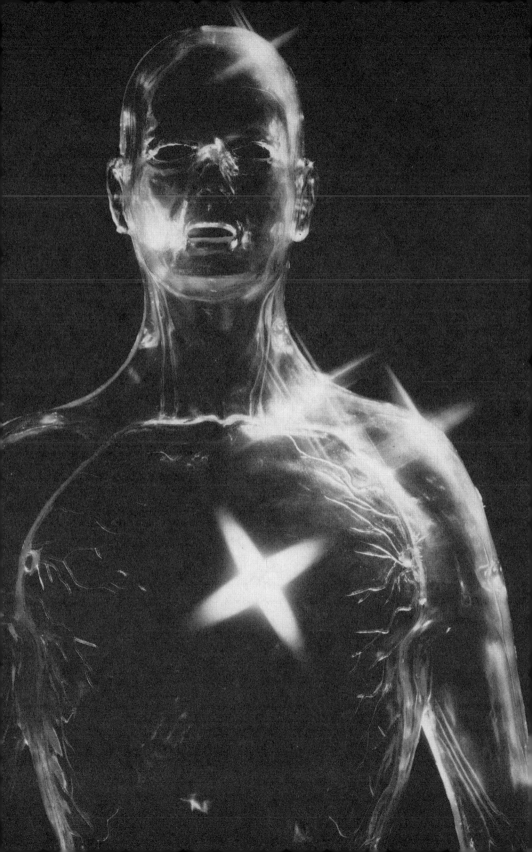

DAY 13 ● EXERCISE 3

**"PSYCHIC
ENERGY
RELEASE"**

MIND DEVELOPMENT

This exercise will help release consciousness which may have been suppressed in you during survival-related incidents. It will also give you a feeling of relaxation and help you develop a healthy body.

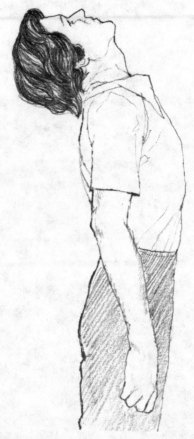

EXERCISE A—The Neck Stretch

With your hands at your sides point your chin upward as far as you can toward the ceiling. Hold it in that position for 5 seconds. Now slowly rotate your neck clockwise until you have brought your chin back to its original starting point. Repeat this exercise 15 times.

EXERCISE B—Reach for the stars

Starting with your hands at your sides, lock your two hands together by placing the thumb of your right hand between the index finger and thumb of your left hand. Now bring your hands above your head and reach as high as you can. With every stretch you will feel the energy released in your body. Hold that position for 15 seconds and repeat four more times.

EXERCISE C—The Windmill

Start with your hands at your sides. Raise and extend
them to your sides so that they are at right angles to your
body. Rotate your arms in the largest circle possible.
Repeat this exercise 60 times.

EXERCISE D—Reverse Windmill

Reverse Exercise #3 so that you start by bringing your
hands backward instead of forward and repeat 60 times.

EXERCISE E—Backward Back Bend

Place your hands on your hips while standing erect and from the lower back upward, bend your body back as far as you can. Repeat 10 times.

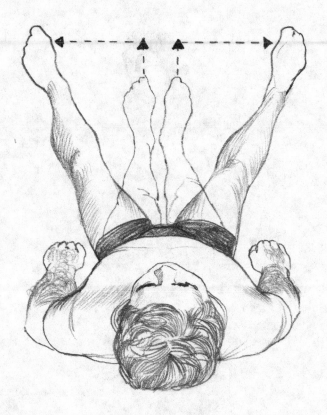

EXERCISE F—Abdominal Stretch

Lie on your back with your hands at your sides, with your feet approximately twelve inches apart. Now lift your legs six inches off the ground and keep them there for 10 seconds. Then extend your legs to the side as far as you can and hold them there for 10 seconds. Next, lift your legs in the air, still extended, as high as you can and hold them there for 10 seconds. Bring your legs back together to the original position six inches off the ground. Repeat 10 times.

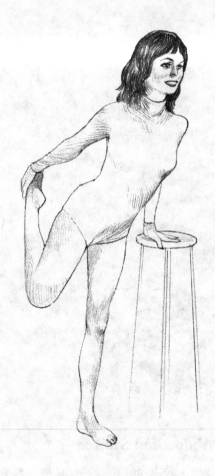

EXERCISE G—Thigh Extension

Place your right hand on your right ankle and your left hand on a chair about three feet high for support. Now take your right hand and right ankle and pull your right leg back as far as you can, holding it for 10 seconds. Repeat 10 times.

Repeat the procedure with your left hand and left ankle.

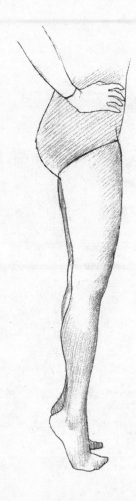

EXERCISE H—Calf Extension

With your hands on your hips, raise up on your toes as high as you possibly can and hold that position for 10 seconds. Repeat 15 times.

EXERCISE I—Facial Stretch

Open your mouth as wide as you can. Hold that position
for 10 seconds. Repeat 15 times.

Most people prefer to do these exercises on a daily basis since the exercises have both calisthenic and Psycho-Calisthenic® benefits. The amount of time you spend on these exercises should depend on both the physical and mental benefits you are seeking.

DAY 13 ● EXERCISE 4

GOAL 1

PROGRAMMING

Enter the Alpha dimension by the 5 to 1 method, the body relaxation method and the 10 to 1 method. Program your first goal.

In addition to entering the Alpha dimension by the above methods and programming your first goal for 10 minutes, use the post-Alpha instructions to gain additional benefits from Alpha programming.

After using the post-Alpha instructions, come out of the Alpha dimension by the 1 to 5 method.

A man said to the universe:
"Sir, I exist!"
"However," replied the universe, "The fact has not created in me a sense of obligation."

STEPHEN CRANE

DAY 14 ● EXERCISE 1

"HOW TO UNDERSTAND PEOPLE"

FUNDAMENTAL FACT OF LIFE

Every day you come into contact with many different people. Your evaluation of the performance, potential, efficiency, and ethics of these people are important factors in your decision-making process about other people and yourself. In a sense you can rate people on an emotional tone scale.

This emotional tone scale includes:

4.0   Enthusiasm (cheerfulness).

3.5   Interest (amusement).

3.0   Conservatism (contentment).

2.5   Boredom.

2.0   Overt hostility.

1.8   Pain.

1.5   Anger.

1.2   Lack of sympathy.

1.1   Covert hostility.

1.0   Fear.

0.9   Sympathy.

0.8   Appeasement.

0.05   Apathy.

The elements of the emotional tone scale can be described as follows:

The better a person is understood, the higher his emotional tone level.

4. What does someone talk about?

People who are achieving their goals enjoy passing on good ideas, concepts, and solutions. Underachievers enjoy talking about and listening to negative ideas and problems.

5. Talk Balance.

People with a high emotional tone level enjoy talking. They are also able and willing to listen. However, when you see someone who is a compulsive talker, you can assume that he is on the lower end of the emotional tone scale.

6. Communication Lag.

Communication lag is the length of time that it takes a person to respond to a question he is asked. If you asked a person with a high emotional tone level a question, such as: "How many windows are there in this room?," he would answer you immediately. However, someone low on the emotional tone scale will hesitate and wait for a long time depending on how depressed he is. He may ask you what you are driving at or ask if it is a trick question.

7. Accidents.

The more accidents a person has, the more frequently he cuts himself, bruises himself, smashes his car and so forth, the lower that person is on the emotional tone scale regardless of how well he explains his tribulations.

8. Doing a Job.

People with a high emotional tone accomplish a great deal in a short time, and people with a low emotional tone take a long time to do a small job.

9. Mobility.

A person with a high emotional tone is more capable of change and flexibility. The person with a lower emotional tone finds change threatening to his belief system and is unable to alter his behavior patterns easily.

10. Generalities.

People with a lower emotional tone level use generalities to justify their thinking. Nobody loves me. Everybody thinks this way. People always, and so forth. People with a high emotional tone level are specific, and their opinions are supported by statistics.

11. Ethics.

The higher the ethics of a person, the higher his emotional tone level.

12. Possessions.

People who take care of themselves, their homes and their possessions are usually operating on a high emotional tone level.

Observe other people and yourself and decide how everyone measures up on the emotional tone scale. Then you will be in a better position to choose your friends and your future.

DAY 14 ● EXERCISE 2

"OTHER MEDITATIVE TECHNIQUES"

DEPROGRAMMING

A number of additional techniques have been developed which subdue the conscious mind so that the images and messages from the unconscious mind can more easily surface.

One of these techniques is the Mantra.

The Mantra is a phrase which is repeated over and over again in meditation. Ken Keyes of the Living Love Center of Berkeley, California, has developed the Mantra "All ways us living love."

Other groups have developed chants as their form of Mantra.

Some groups have developed meditative techniques such as placing an index finger in each ear and concentrating on the ringing sound and vibration which is generated, or bringing the tongue backward into the mouth reaching back as far as possible and concentrating on the taste sensation which is generated.

The purpose of all these techniques is to distract the conscious self, by limiting your sensory inputs, in order to become aware of the images and sensations that are flowing from the subconscious mind to the conscious mind. Select the meditative technique which is most effective for you.

DAY 14 ● EXERCISE 3

"PSYCHIC
ENERGY
RELEASE"

MIND DEVELOPMENT EXERCISES

"Psychic Energy Release." Repeat all the exercises —
from Day 13, Exercise 3.

These exercises will help release consciousness which
may have been suppressed in you during survival-related
incidents. It will also give you a feeling of relaxation and
help you develop a healthy body.

DAY 14 • EXERCISE 4

GOAL 1
PROGRAMMING

Enter the Alpha dimension by the 5 to 1 method, the body relaxation method and the 10 to 1 method. Program your first goal.

In addition to entering the Alpha dimension by the above methods and programming your first goal for 10 minutes, use the post-Alpha instructions to gain additional benefits from Alpha programming.

After using the post-Alpha instructions, come out of the Alpha dimension by the 1 to 5 method.

CHAPTER

5

THE THIRD WEEK

SPECIAL INSTRUCTIONS:

1. Do not read more than what is required for each day.

2. Each day there are four exercises. Do not substitute. Perform the exercises just as they are listed.

3. Do not be lazy and try to redo the exercise from memory. If you are not sure of an exercise, go back and reread it.

4. Each Fundamental Fact of Life should be read three times. Then close your eyes and reflect upon its significance as it relates to you. In total, you will spend approximately 30 minutes each day with your Psycho-Calisthenics® program.

5. On the next page is a Psycho-Calisthenics Program Chart for the third week. But be sure to read the exercises and do them one day at a time.

6. Note the space at the left of the chart for the date and comment. Write down anything you think is significant.

PSYCHO-CALISTHENICS ® PROGRAM CHART—WEEK 3

DAY 15 DATE: COMMENT:..	Creating a Detailed Life Program
DAY 16 DATE: COMMENT:..	The Brain Trust Theory
DAY 17 DATE: COMMENT:..	The Concept of Time Conservation
DAY 18 DATE: COMMENT:..	The Concept of Attention Units
DAY 19 DATE: COMMENT:..	Mental Toughness
DAY 20 DATE: COMMENT:..	Persistence
DAY 21 DATE: COMMENT:..	Cycle Completion

DEPROGRAMMING	MIND DEVELOPMENT	PROGRAMMING
Self Analysis	Technique of Auditory Evocation	Goal 1
Self Analysis	Technique of Auditory Evocation	Goal 1
Self Analysis	Projection Into Objects, Animals and Other People	Goal 1
Self Analysis	Projection Into Objects, Animals and Other People	Goal 1
Present Time Problem List	Techniques of Imaginative Evocation of Other Sensations	Goal 1
Dream Log	Techniques of Imaginative Evocation of Other Sensations	Goal 1
Cancel, Cancel Technique	The Technique of the Ideal Model	Goal 1

DAY 15 ● EXERCISE 1

"CREATING A DETAILED LIFE PROGRAM"

FUNDAMENTAL FACT OF LIFE

If you are going to be successful in reaching your goals, you must draw up a blueprint for achieving them. Suppose your goal is to find a person you can truly love and share your life and happiness with. That is an acceptable objective, but it is not a self-fulfilling prophecy. Very few people ever make a really detailed plan to find someone to love.

Women sit near their telephone waiting for Prince Charming to materialize in a flash of cosmic consciousness. Men who have an opportunity to be more agressive, generally do not take advantage of the opportunity. Most young men seeking women limit themselves to following attractive ladies with their eyes as they walk down the street, or perhaps mustering enough nerve for a whistle or provocative comment.

There are many ways a man can meet a woman under favorable circumstances, including:

1. Being introduced by a mutual friend.

2. Coming into contact with a woman during the day, for example, while walking down the street, traveling, sitting in a restaurant or at a resort or club.

3. Specifically choosing a woman that he is not acquainted with but with whom he would like to spend some time and arranging to contact her.

4. Putting an ad in the personal column to reach women who share his interests.

At first this orderly approach to falling in love may violate your sensibilities. Love, you say, is supposed to be a natural thing, something ordained by your horoscope. It just is not so. All things in life that you want to achieve require a detailed plan.

In developing the blueprint, you must open yourself to all forms of actions and not exclude a possibility without thinking about it. You might rule out putting an ad in a newspaper because it is incompatible with your belief system. However, if you do not use an ad, the probability of finding your someone is generally decreased.

You must learn to be a researcher and a writer in organizing your plan. Seek out the necessary data you need to implement your idea. Write your plan out in detail and by keeping a picture of the plan in your mind's eye, you will heighten the probability of the plan's success.

Writing your plan is the first symbolic and functional step in converting an idea into a reality.

If your plan is unsuccessful, try again. One of the characteristics of successful men is that they have learned from their failures, reshaped their plans and achieved success.

DAY 15 • EXERCISE 2

"SELF ANALYSIS"

DEPROGRAMMING

—This list will help you perceive the motion of people and objects. Can you remember when:

Something pleasant moved very fast.

You saw somebody you didn't like running away from you.

You enjoyed seeing the rain fall.

You enjoyed seeing children play.

You saw a brook flowing.

You saw a kite flying.

You were exhilarated while riding downhill.

You saw a bird fly gracefully.

You scared an animal and it moved away from you.

You watched a graceful girl.

You broke something you didn't like.

You watched a graceful man.

You enjoyed watching a ferocious animal.

You watched something going around in circles.

You were happy to see something shoot up in the air.

You watched a fast horse.

You saw a "shooting star."

You saw somebody you liked walking toward you.

You lifted an object.

You watched a glowing fire.

DAY 15 ● EXERCISE 3

"TECHNIQUE OF AUDITORY EVOCATION"

MIND DEVELOPMENT

This exercise is similar to the exercise in visualization.

Try to duplicate the following sounds in your mind, by imagining you hear them.

1. The first group of sounds are the sounds of nature. They include:

The sea.

Waves crashing on rocks.

A waterfall.

The wind whispering in a forest.

The rain.

Thunderstorm.

2. Other sounds are man-made. They include:

A Rock 'n Roll band.

An orchestra.

A hammer hammering on a wall.

A car horn.

A doorbell.

DAY 15 ● EXERCISE 4

GOAL 1

PROGRAMMING

Enter the Alpha dimension by the 5 to 1 method, the body relaxation method and the 10 to 1 method. Program your first goal.

In addition to entering the Alpha dimension by the above methods and programming your first goal for 10 minutes, use the post-Alpha instructions to gain additional bene-fits from Alpha programming.

After using the post-Alpha instructions, come out of the Alpha dimension by the 1 to 5 method.

DAY 16 ● EXERCISE 1

"THE BRAIN TRUST THEORY"

FUNDAMENTAL FACT OF LIFE

In order to achieve your goals in life a detailed life blueprint is the first step. The principal by-product of a detailed life blueprint is the realization that you need other people to achieve your goals.

If you are a businessman seeking financial success, you need an accountant, a lawyer, and an advertising professional to help you in achieving your business goals. You must supplement your own skills by finding people in the areas of sales, finance, and marketing. You must. also surround yourself with people who share common goals and who can help you achieve your goals. These people are your personal "BRAIN TRUST."

You must actively seek these people out. Decide what you have to offer to these people in return for their contributions to your goals. Motivation is critical in gaining their assistance and performance.

Arrange to meet with your brain trust on a regular basis, so that you will have an opportunity to jointly perfect and achieve your goals.

Your brain trust can be as fundamental as three young ladies deciding together on how to find a man to love or as complicated as a group of scientists deciding the procedures needed to put a man on the moon.

You must learn to keep harmony between yourself and every member of your brain trust. The oneness of purpose and the exchange of love energy between you and your brain trust will have a positive effect on your chances of success. Develop a detailed plan using your brain trust and learn to manage time to your best advantage.

DAY 16 ● EXERCISE 2

"SELF ANALYSIS"
DEPROGRAMMING

This list will help you recall bodily sensations.

Can you remember when:

You enjoyed just sitting.

You put your toe in your mouth.

You tried to stand on your head.

You tried to see if you could be a contortionist.

You ate an excellent meal.

You drove a good car.

Someone admired your body.

You enthusiastically stood up to go some place.

DAY 16 ● EXERCISE 3

"TECHNIQUE OF AUDITORY EVOCATION"

MIND DEVELOPMENT

Repeat Day 15, Exercise 3, "Technique of Auditory Evocation." This is the second time you are doing this exercise.

This exercise is similar to the exercise in visualization.

Try to duplicate the following sounds in your mind, by imagining you hear them.

1. The first group of sounds are the sounds of nature. They include:

The sea.

Waves crashing on rocks.

A waterfall.

The wind whispering in a forest.

The rain.

Thunderstorm.

2. Other sounds are man-made. They include:

A rock 'n Roll band.

An orchestra.

A hammer hammering on a wall.

A car horn.

A doorbell.

DAY 16 ● EXERCISE 4

GOAL 1

PROGRAMMING

Enter the Alpha dimension by the 5 to 1 method, the body relaxation method and the 10 to 1 method. Program your first goal.

In addition to entering the Alpha dimension by the above methods and programming your first goal for 10 minutes, use the post-Alpha instructions to gain additional benefits from Alpha programming.

After using the post-Alpha instructions, come out of the Alpha dimension by the 1 to 5 method.

DAY 17 ● EXERCISE 1

"THE CONCEPT OF TIME CONSERVATION" FUNDAMENTAL FACT OF LIFE

In every day, there are 24 hours, 1440 minutes and 86,400 seconds, no more, no less. We all must operate within this time frame. If you want to achieve your goals, you must manage this time well.

We all have habits or behavior patterns that have become automatic, and we are the victims of our programmed behavior. We have become a servant of our behavior instead of its master.

When was the last time you asked yourself, "How much time do I lose in the morning by not having my clothing and breakfast planned? When was the last time I reexamined the way I travel to work?" Have you asked yourself recently what meetings, what people, what circumstances, would be better avoided in order to acquire more time?

Time can be acquired by detailed planning. Eliminate things in life that are wasting your time and sapping your energy. Control your environment. For example, you probably assume that you need so many hours of sleep. If someone asked how many hours of sleep you need, you might say eight each night. The kind of bed you will sleep in and the temperature of the room could improve your sleep. You may find that eight hours of sleep are really not necessary. People who have practiced Psycho-Calisthenics®, can often be completely rested after six hours of sleep or less. By eliminating unnecessary sleep, you can add minutes and hours to your day.

If you are presently sleeping eight hours a night, within one month of the initiation of your Psycho-Calisthenics® program, you may only require approximately six hours sleep. By investing half an hour a day you would obtain a 300% dividend in time to add to the pursuit of your goals.

If you want to live in the present you will have more of the present to live in by managing your time better.

DAY 17 • EXERCISE 2

"SELF ANALYSIS"

DEPROGRAMMING

This list will help you recall specific experiences in which you achieved an objective.

Can you remember when:

You threw something in the air.

You walked downstairs.

You acquired something you wanted.

You were proud that you could move something heavy.

You handled your energy well.

You built a fire.

You spent time pleasantly.

You were master of your own time.

You changed something for the better.

You brought somebody you liked close to you.

You brought a number of pleasant objects together.

You tore an unwanted object to pieces.

You held an object close that you wanted.

You emptied a space you wanted.

You realized you were living your own life.

You escaped from a dangerous place.

A man is rich in proportion to the number of things he can afford to let alone.
HENRY DAVID THOREAU

DAY 17 • EXERCISE 3

"PROJECTION INTO OBJECTS, ANIMALS AND OTHER PEOPLE"

MIND DEVELOPMENT

In order to gain greater harmony with your environment and to develop your mental skills, learn to project your consciousness into objects, animals and other people. Enter the Alpha dimension and project your consciousness into the following:

Enter a wall. Feel the plaster and density of the molecules. Sense the hardness of the wall as your consciousness penetrates it. Experience this for 30 seconds.

Enter the body of your favorite animal. Feel the beating of its heart and its breathing. Sense the warmth and flow of the blood and feel the pulsating life within the animal. Be there for 30 seconds.

Project yourself into your favorite flower. Sense the special fragrance, feel the softness of the petals. Let yourself feel the relative size of the flower and you. Imagine a complete outdoor setting for the flower. Experience it for 30 seconds.

Project yourself into a bar of gold. Feel the coldness and smoothness. Feel the density of the molecules. Experience it for 30 seconds.

Project yourself into an ear of corn. Feel the ridges of the kernels as you enter into the center of the corn. Taste the sweetness and freshness of the corn. Experience it for 30 seconds.

Project yourself into the body of the person you love the most. Feel the warmth as you enter their body. Feel the love. Feel all the organs, the heart, liver, stomach, and lungs. Be there in that person for 30 seconds.

As you practice this exercise you will develop strong, visual impressions and develop greater insight into the projected object of your consciousness.

DAY 17 • EXERCISE 4

GOAL 1

PROGRAMMING

Enter the Alpha dimension by the 5 to 1 method, the body relaxation method and the 10 to 1 method. Program your first goal.

In addition to entering the Alpha dimension by the above methods and programming your first goal for 10 minutes, use the post-Alpha instructions to gain additional benefits from Alpha programming.

After using the post-Alpha instructions, come out of the Alpha dimension by the 1 to 5 method.

DAY 18 ● EXERCISE 1

"THE CONCEPT OF ATTENTION UNITS"

FUNDAMENTAL FACT OF LIFE

Think of your mind as a vast computer consisting of three programming devices—the subconscious, the conscious, and the superconscious (your spiritual self).

For the purpose of this analogy, imagine that each of these programming devices has a magnetic tape reel and that one thousand units of data can be stored and attended to simultaneously.

As the programmer of your own computer, you may choose to put nonsense or important data into each of your magnetic tape reels; so decide what is relevant and what is not. Simply stated, the idea of attention units means that if you clutter your mental computer with nonsense you reduce your power and potential.

One major purpose of Psycho-Calisthenics® is to have you take responsibility for what you put into your mental computer. Psycho-Calisthenics® will also help you select the most important data for your goals.

For instance, if you divert 200 units of your attention to thinking about a love affair that went wrong, then you have diminished the power of your computer. Choose what you will think about. Decide what is important to you and discard data which detracts from your ability to live in the present.

DAY 18 • EXERCISE 2

"SELF ANALYSIS"
DEPROGRAMMING

This list will help your memory.

Can you remember a time when:

You did something else with the time which was appointed for another purpose.

You were happy to have acquired something you couldn't afford.

You happily defied directions you had been given.

You were sent to one place and went to another.

You chose your own clothing.

You wore something in spite of what people thought.

You got rid of something that bored you.

You were glad to have to choose between two objects.

You didn't drink any more than you really wanted to.

You didn't read a book you had been given.

You refused to be used by someone.

You slept where you pleased.

You found you had been right in refusing something.

DAY 18 • EXERCISE 3

"PROJECTION INTO OBJECTS, ANIMALS AND OTHER PEOPLE"

MIND DEVELOPMENT

Reread Day 17, Exercise 3 and repeat the entire exercise.

In order to gain greater harmony with your environment and to develop your mental skills, learn to project your consciousness into objects, animals and other people. Enter the Alpha dimension and project your consciousness into the following:

Enter a wall. Feel the plaster and density of the molecules. Sense the hardness of the wall as your consciousness penetrates it. Experience this for 30 seconds.

Enter the body of your favorite animal. Feel the beating of its heart and its breathing. Sense the warmth and flow of the blood and feel the pulsating life within the animal. Be there for 30 seconds.

Project yourself into your favorite flower. Sense the special fragrance, feel the softness of the petals. Let yourself feel the relative size of the flower and you. Imagine a complete outdoor setting for the flower. Experience it for 30 seconds.

Project yourself into a bar of gold. Feel the coldness and smoothness. Feel the density of the molecules. Experience it for 30 seconds.

Project yourself into an ear of corn. Feel the ridges of the kernels as you enter into the center of the corn. Taste the sweetness and freshness of the corn. Experience it 30 seconds.

Project yourself into the body of the person you love the most. Feel the warmth as you enter their body. Feel the love. Feel all the organs, the heart, liver, stomach, and lungs. Be there in that person for 60 seconds.

As you practice this exercise you will develop strong, visual impressions and develop greater insight into the projected object of your consciousness.

DAY 18 • EXERCISE 4

GOAL 1

PROGRAMMING

Enter the Alpha dimension by the 5 to 1 method, the body relaxation method and the 10 to 1 method. Program your first goal.

In addition to entering the Alpha dimension by the above methods and programming your first goal for 10 minutes, use the post-Alpha instructions to gain additional benefits from Alpha programming.

After using the post-Alpha instructions, come out of the Alpha dimension by the 1 to 5 method.

DAY 19 ● EXERCISE 1

"MENTAL TOUGHNESS"

FUNDAMENTAL FACT OF LIFE

There are more than three billion people on this planet, each with their own goals, whether clearly or vaguely defined. Each is in a different stage of development and many will attempt to achieve their purpose in life to the detriment of your own goals.

That is why you must learn to develop Mental Toughness.

Acquire the necessary data about yourself so that you can clearly define your goals. Try to achieve your goal in a loving way, without feeling angry when another person thwarts your purpose. You must acquire mental toughness so that you will not be swayed from your purpose even though others try to manipulate you to achieve their purposes.

There is a fine line between mental toughness and inflexibility. You must be goal-oriented without being rigid.

Avoid people who interfere with your goals. As you acquire greater ability, you will learn to pursue your own goals and simultaneously help others with their purposes and goals.

DAY 19 ● EXERCISE 2

"PRESENT TIME PROBLEM LIST"

MIND DEVELOPMENT EXERCISES

Make a list of all those problems you presently have. There may be 20 problems or 2,000. On the left side of a piece of paper list all these problems, allowing at least eight lines underneath each problem. On the right side of each piece of paper write the solutions to these problems, after you develop them while in the Alpha dimension.

Get yourself into a relaxed state and enter the Alpha dimension by the 5 to 1 method, the body relaxation method, and 10 to 1 method. Remove all barriers from your thinking. Limiting attitudes about what is possible and what is not possible must be erased.

With each problem, imagine yourself in the center of a vast circle of alternatives and view each alternative, no matter how preposterous that alternative may initially seem. Devote enough time to each problem until you feel you have no more possibilities for solving it and then go on to the next problem.

The first time you do this exercise, you may only solve 10 to 20% of your problems or maybe you will solve 80 to 90% of them, but whatever you do it will begin to remove the burden of unhappiness which you have placed on your shoulders.

DAY 19 ● EXERCISE 3

"TECHNIQUES OF IMAGINATIVE EVOCATION OF OTHER SENSATIONS"

MIND DEVELOPMENT

The sense of touch, taste, and smell are additional senses which you can develop. They can help you increase your imagination and your ability to visualize and achieve results.

Imagine tasting the following:

1. Salt.
2. Sugar.
3. Lemon.
4. Pickle.
5. Carbonated water.
6. An apple.
7. Steak.
8. Butter.
9. Lettuce.
10. Hot soup.
11. Frozen ice cream.
12. Foul tasting medicine.
13. Water.
14. Liquor.
15. Cigarettes.
16. Metallic taste of a fork.
17. Hot peppers.
18. Raw fish.
19. Peanuts.
20. Rye bread.

DAY 19 • EXERCISE 4

GOAL 1
PROGRAMMING

Enter the Alpha dimension by the 5 to 1 method, the body relaxation method and the 10 to 1 method. Program your first goal.

In addition to entering the Alpha dimension by the above methods and programming your first goal for 10 minutes, use the post-Alpha instructions to gain additional benefits from Alpha programming.

After using the post-Alpha instructions, come out of the Alpha dimension by the 1 to 5 method.

DAY 20 • EXERCISE 1

"PERSISTENCE"

FUNDAMENTAL FACT OF LIFE

It is not enough to formulate a plan and implement it only on a casual basis. Persistence is important once a goal has been clearly defined. Persistence is the act of doing until you achieve your goal.

Persistence can be as limited as cleaning a spot from a rug until the rug is like new or as complicated as building a 100-story office complex involving years and the interaction and talents of thousands of people.

Many books have been written about persistence and the concept may have been discussed with sufficient repetition that it generates an "Oh really, I know that" reaction. But examine your life and see where, with a little more persistence, you could have achieved more than you did.

Was it the marriage that with just a slightly greater effort you could have saved? Was it the sales call that with greater persistence and enthusiasm could have been successful?

Unconditional, unwavering, undaunted, undeniable purpose. Do it, do it, do it, do it—Now, now, now, now, now.

DAY 20 • EXERCISE 2

"DREAM LOG"

MIND DEVELOPMENT EXERCISES

Keep an 8½x11 spiral bound notebook next to your bed.

When you awaken from a dream, immediately have a pen available, your dream log book, and a light that is not too bright so that it does not trigger you too abruptly back to full consciousness. A tape recorder next to your bed is another method of recording dreams. They can be transcribed later.

Your dreams should be written down by bits of information or by concept, rather than sentences and paragraphs.

For instance:

> I was walking
>
> down
>
> a dark corridor
>
> a blue
>
> tiger
>
> suddenly
>
> sprang at me
>
> I was afraid
>
> I began to run
>
> I woke up

DAY 20 EXERCISE 2 (con't.)

You should take each piece of information and examine it in order to obtain the fullest meaning of your dream. The subconscious mind deals in generalities. To the subconscious mind a dark corridor could be a journey of uncertainty, a subway train, sleep, or being in your mother's womb. They may all be symbols that are used interchangeably.

In order to best understand your dreams, make an association list for each of those items. Enter into your dream log any insights you have into your dream.

If the significance of a tiger is unclear to you, ask yourself, "What do I associate a tiger with? Is a tiger an aggressive person? A cat? Or is a tiger a stuffed toy I had when I was a child?"

By examining each bit of data you will be better able to understand your own associations.

There are endless theories on dreams. It is my belief, however, that dreams are part of a communication system between the unconscious, superconscious, and conscious minds. The language of the unconscious mind is one of generalities and you must learn to interpret this language in order to understand yourself.

You can experiment by setting your clock for 30, 60, 90 or 120 minutes from the time you think you will fall asleep to determine where you find your most significant dreams. These dreams may be different in character and composition from those dreams right before waking.

Many people believe they do not dream, but in fact it is only that they do not remember their dreams.

There is vital data to be obtained about your unconscious mind, its associations and fears by analyzing your dreams. This is a technique that you can successfully do by yourself and because each subconscious has its own language, only you can analyze your own dreams.

DAY 20 ● EXERCISE 3

"IMAGINATIVE EVOCATION"

MIND DEVELOPMENT

Refer to Day 19, Exercise 3 and repeat the entire exercise.

The sense of touch, taste, and smell are additional senses which you can develop. They can help you increase your imagination and your ability to visualize and achieve results.

Imagine tasting the following:

1. Salt.
2. Sugar.
3. Lemon.
4. Pickle.
5. Carbonated water.
6. An apple.
7. Steak.
8. Butter.
9. Lettuce.
10. Hot soup.
11. Frozen ice cream.
12. Foul tasting medicine.
13. Water.
14. Liquor.
15. Cigarettes.
16. Metallic taste of a fork.
17. Hot peppers.
18. Raw fish.
19. Peanuts.
20. Rye bread.

DAY 20 ● EXERCISE 4

GOAL 1
PROGRAMMING

Enter the Alpha dimension by the 5 to 1 method, the body relaxation method and the 10 to 1 method. Program your first goal.

In addition to entering the Alpha dimension by the above methods and programming your first goal for 10 minutes, use the post-Alpha instructions to gain additional benefits from Alpha programming.

After using the post-Alpha instructions, come out of the Alpha dimension by the 1 to 5 method.

DAY 21 ● EXERCISE 1

"CYCLE COMPLETION"

FUNDAMENTAL FACT OF LIFE

To confront your problems and accomplish your detailed life blueprint you must complete cycles of action, inter-action, or communication and not constantly leave loose ends dangling. If your goal is to improve your house, you will find your goals less likely to be achieved if you simul-taneously undertake 15 miscellaneous projects instead of concentrating on one or two important projects at a time.

If you are a salesman you can define your market area and select the most significant prospects. Approach these prospects on an orderly basis, completing each cycle by either making them customers or putting them on your follow-up list.

After you have completed a cycle you remove it from your mind, thereby allowing yourself time for new cycles. As you learn to rapidly and efficiently complete cycles, you will find the pleasure you derive increases accordingly. The more cycles you complete, the more you will be tak-ing responsibility for your own life.

DAY 21 ● EXERCISE 2

"CANCEL, CANCEL TECHNIQUE"

DEPROGRAMMING

Jose Silva has developed the "Cancel, Cancel" technique.

Simply stated, the Cancel, Cancel technique says that since the subconscious mind is constantly being programmed, it is natural and logical to assume that one would want to remove from the subconscious any programming errors.

For example, if you have an argument with your secretary and you say "Eva is really a pain in the neck," you are making an associative pairing in your subconscious that Eva equals a pain in the neck.

With enough repetition and emotional charge, the sight of Eva may begin to cause a pain in the neck.

The "Cancel, Cancel" technique says that when you are aware of your behavior and you realize that you have programmed an error which is not beneficial to you, merely by saying the phrase "Cancel, Cancel," you are removing that program and telling your subconscious that this was a "key punching" error and should be withdrawn from your data bank.

You may make a statement that you would like to withdraw, for example, "I hope that Bob drops dead." Or, "I am always making mistakes." These statements represent negative programming and should be removed by the "Cancel, Cancel" technique.

To amplify the success of the "Cancel, Cancel" technique, enter the Alpha dimension by the 5 to 1 method, the body relaxation method, and the 10 to 1 method, and say to yourself: In the future when I want to remove a program that has been placed in my unconscious within the previous five minutes, I will say, "Cancel, Cancel," and my unconscious mind will remove this fact from my programming.

This technique allows you to deprogram those things which were generally experienced within the previous five minutes. The closer to the event, the greater the likelihood of easily removing the programming.

DAY 21 ● EXERCISE 3

"THE TECHNIQUE OF THE IDEAL MODEL"

MIND DEVELOPMENT

This exercise will help you to achieve your goals. To do this you can use a person whom you respect in each of the areas as a model for you to emulate.

1. Visualize exactly the person you would like to be. Create a physical image of yourself including height, weight, facial expression, features, and clothing.

2. If you know a person who is a model of the person you would like to resemble, mentally measure that person next to your ideal picture of yourself and adjust your image to match the "Ideal Model."

3. Now create a personality that is an ideal model for you. Remember that you are flexible and tell yourself that you can be whatever you choose to be in life by acquiring the behavior and personality you desire.

4. Now imagine a picture of a .very healthy person. Imagine the healthy lungs and heart, steady breathing, the flow of blood through your system. Feel health pulsating through your body. It is your mind that governs your health.

5. Visualize someone, who is especially healthy, you would want to be like. Imagine their physical radiance and duplicate that radiance in yourself.

6. Now imagine yourself in the occupation that best suits you. Imagine performing duties in that role. Sense the feeling of being that person and making that your role.

7. Now visualize someone who has that job and whose performance you would like to duplicate. Sense his knowledge, his experience, his physical bearing. Be that person and adjust your ideal to be like that person.

Begin to act like your ideal model. Think of yourself as handsome and you will feel that you can behave confidently. Assure yourself that you can be healthy. Convince yourself that you can acquire enough experience to get the job you want. If you hold your model in your mind, you will begin to be the person you want to be.

Your life is limited only by the boundaries you establish for yourself.

DAY 21 ● EXERCISE 4

GOAL 1

PROGRAMMING

Enter the Alpha dimension by the 5 to 1 method, the body relaxation method and the 10 to 1 method. Program your first goal.

In addition to entering the Alpha dimension by the above methods and programming your first goal for 10 minutes, use the post-Alpha instructions to gain additional benefits from Alpha programming.

After using the post-Alpha instructions, come out of the Alpha dimension by the 1 to 5 method.

CHAPTER

6

THE FOURTH WEEK

SPECIAL INSTRUCTIONS:

1. Do not read more than what is required for each day.

2. Each day there are four exercises. Do not substitute. Perform the exercises just as they are listed.

3. Do not be lazy and try to redo the exercise from memory. If you are not sure of an exercise, go back and reread it.

4. Each Fundamental Fact of Life should be read three times. Then close your eyes and reflect upon its significance as it relates to you. In total, you will spend approximately 30 minutes each day with your Psycho-Calisthenics program.

5. On the next page is a Psycho-Calisthenics® Program Chart for the fourth week. But be sure to read the exercises and do them one day at a time.

6. Note the space at the left of the chart for the date and comment. Write down anything you think is significant.

Reach for the stars . . . at least you won't come up with a handful of mud.
LEO BURNETT AGENCY

PSYCHO-CALISTHENICS ® PROGRAM CHART—WEEK 4

FUNDAMENTAL FACT

DAY 22 DATE: COMMENT:...	Creative Criticism
DAY 23 DATE: COMMENT:...	The Concept of Ethics
DAY 24 DATE: COMMENT:...	Needs & Purposes
DAY 25 DATE: COMMENT:...	Acknowledgement & Validation
DAY 26 DATE: COMMENT:...	The Stable Datum Concept
DAY 27 DATE: COMMENT:...	The Games People Play
DAY 28 DATE: COMMENT:...	The Pygmalion Principle

DEPROGRAMMING	MIND DEVELOPMENT	PROGRAMMING
Self Analysis	Imaginative Evocation of Other Sensations (touching)	Goals 1 & 2
Self Analysis	Imaginative Evocation of Other Sensations (touching)	Goals 1 & 2
Self Analysis	Imaginative Evocation of Other Sensations (smelling)	Goals 1 & 2
Self Analysis	Imaginative Evocation of Other Sensations (smelling)	Goals 1 & 2
Restimulator Log	Deep Breathing	Goals 1 & 2
Emotional Overload	Deep Breathing	Goals 1 & 2
Reducing Conditioned Reflexes	The Exercise of Dictionary Look-up	Goals 1 & 2

New opinions are always suspected, and usually opposed, without any other reason but because they are not already common.

JOHN LOCKE

DAY 22 • EXERCISE 1

"CREATIVE CRITICISM"

FUNDAMENTAL FACT OF LIFE

People vary in their ability to accept reality and in the need they have to defend their behavior. Some people can accept criticism graciously, others cannot.

If someone says to you "I really don't like what you're wearing. It is baggy on you and the color is hideous", you might fly into a rage, pout or feel rejected. If it is said as demonstrated below, it will have a positive effect.

It is important to find ways to constructively criticize people when you feel the criticism is valid.

Creative criticism means criticizing without damaging your relationship.

1. First, give the person you want to criticize three positive statements of agreement.

2. Then, state your criticism.

3. Tell the person how you feel.

4. Tell the person what you want.

For example:

1a "Mary, you are a beautiful woman."

1b "God has favored you with a charming figure."

1c "You have a lively personality which is attractive to everyone."

2. But the dress you have on is the wrong color and it really looks baggy on you."

3. "I feel that you are going to look foolish with that dress on."

4. "I want you to wear another dress."

Another example might be:

1a "Bill, you are a very considerate man."

1b "You are always a stimulating conversationalist."

1c "Your knowledge of psychology is really helpful to me."

2. "But your constant lateness in coming to call for me is unfair."

3. "I feel angry when I sit around wasting time waiting for you."

4. "I want you to call for me on time."

Introduce three validations, then make your criticism. Tell someone how you honestly feel, then tell them exactly what you want. Now you can criticize without damaging the positive communications you share with that person. You are actually adding more agreement than you are taking away.

It is important to think enough of yourself so that creative criticism will not shatter your ego. If someone tells you your pants are ripped in the back, it is much better to accept the comment and repair or change your pants, than to wander through life with your posterior exposed to the world, figuratively speaking.

DAY 22 ● EXERCISE 2

"SELF ANALYSIS"

DEPROGRAMMING

Can you remember when:

You realized someone had been faithful.

You realized you didn't have to be afraid of someone anymore.

You discovered you had few enemies.

You found someone you had been looking for.

You decided to stick something out to the end.

You forbade someone to come near you and they obeyed you.

People thought you were generous.

You helped a friend.

Somebody tossed you up in the air.

You outfoxed an enemy.

You hurt someone you needed.

You made someone you didn't like impatient.

People thought you were interesting.

You took a pleasant trip.

You made someone happy.

You overcame a desire to kill.

You first kissed.

You were late and it didn't matter.

DAY 22 • EXERCISE 3

"IMAGINATIVE EVOCATION OF OTHER SENSATIONS"

MIND DEVELOPMENT

Now imagine touching:

Wool.

Silk.

Wood.

Metal.

Sandpaper.

A jagged piece of glass.

Cold water.

Warm water.

Your own genitals.

Someone else's genitals.

A flower.

Sand.

A hot stove.

A wet sponge.

Felt.

Blood.

DAY 22 • EXERCISE 4

PROGRAMMING

Enter the Alpha dimension by the 5 to 1 method, the body relaxation method, and the 10 to 1 method. Program your first goals.

After programming your first goal for 10 minutes, introduce a second goal and program that for approximately five to ten minutes. (If you already are programming 2 goals, now add a third.) Use the post-Alpha instructions to gain additional benefits from Alpha programming.

After using the post-Alpha instructions, come out of the Alpha dimension by the 1 to 5 method.

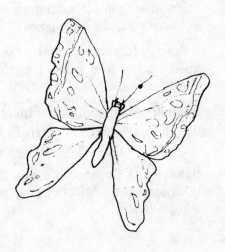

It is the greatest good to the greatest number which is the measure of right and wrong.

JEREMY BENTHAM

DAY 23 ● EXERCISE 1

"THE CONCEPT OF ETHICS"

FUNDAMENTAL FACT OF LIFE

Ethics can be defined as behavior which causes the maximum amount of good for the maximum number of people.

Ethics are not to be confused with morality, which is a group of beliefs which change from society to society and even day to day.

It is unethical to selfishly enforce your wants and desires upon other people taking away their pleasure in order to achieve your own pleasure.

Behavior is more ethical to the extent that it maximizes good and is less ethical to the extent that it minimizes good.

Behavior is innocuously ethical if you sit in your room and watch television. You derive pleasure and no one is made to suffer (unless you play the television too loudly).

Behavior is dynamically ethical when you turn off your television set, get out of your room, and visit a sick friend who is lonely.

Behavior is innocuously unethical when you take the last apple in the refrigerator instead of giving the apple to someone who might like it more than you do.

Behavior is dynamically unethical if you add poison to the apple because you think someone is conspiring against you.

Each of us has in our subconscious mind an idea of ethical and unethical behavior.

For instance, we may unconsciously associate ethical behavior with someone who looks you straight in the eye, someone who responds to your questions promptly and completely or someone who has not acquired nervous gestures.

On a subconscious level these criteria of ethical behavior are continually run through your subconscious computer and give you a "gut feeling" about the ethics of the individual with whom you are dealing. If the programs in your subconscious computer are based on valid data, you will be a so-called "good judge of character."

Your superconscious mind is hooked into a universal data bank which has all answers to all questions. If you become loving and at one with the world then you can tap your superconscious data bank and quickly and correctly determine the ethics of the individual with whom you are interacting.

Unethical people will eventually be found out because they emit warning signals to the subconscious and super-conscious of the people they deal with.

The concept of ethics says: If you are ethical, you add to the positive vibrations in this world. Others will perceive your goodness on a subconscious and superconscious level and thus help you achieve your goals in life. If you add to the negative vibrations in life, others will perceive your bad intentions on a subconscious and supercon-scious level and they will avoid helping you achieve your goals.

Ethics is something each person decides for himself. Gen-erally speaking, people consider it unethical to have an affair that breaks up a marriage, to keep money that does not belong to you, or to bug telephones. However, some examples are not so clearcut. If you want to date someone on a certain evening and you know that another fellow had made the date to take the girl out to dinner, a show and dancing, would it be unethical for you to get the girl to break the date to go out with you?

DAY 23 • EXERCISE 2

"SELF ANALYSIS"

DEPROGRAMMING

Can you remember when:

You caught an enemy in a lie.

You and your friends enjoyed life.

You were happy to listen to someone.

You overcame someone bigger than you.

You made someone glad to be alive.

You found love really existed.

Your luck was good.

You received pleasant mail.

You knew a good man.

Somebody imitated your manner.

There was danger and you were ready.

Somebody unexpectedly reappeared.

You discovered your regrets were in vain.

You were considered remarkable.

You repeated something and weren't sorry for it.

Somebody said you resembled someone you liked.

You restored a friendship.

You tried to save somebody you disliked from ruin.

You were happy to find someone wasn't what he seemed.

You found you really cared about others.

You found a person wasn't as severe as you had thought.

DAY 23 ● EXERCISE 3

"IMAGINATIVE
EVOCATION
OF OTHER
SENSATIONS"

MIND DEVELOPMENT

Refer to Day 22, Exercise 3 and repeat the exercise.

Now imagine touching:

Wool.

Silk.

Wood.

Metal.

Sandpaper.

A jagged piece of glass.

Cold water.

Warm water.

Your own genitals.

Someone else's genitals.

A flower.

Sand.

A hot stove.

A wet sponge.

Felt.

Blood.

DAY 23 ● EXERCISE 4

GOAL 1 & 2

PROGRAMMING

Enter the Alpha dimension by the 5 to 1 method, the body relaxation method, and the 10 to 1 method. Program your first goals.

After programming your first goal for 10 minutes, introduce a second goal and program that for approximately five to ten minutes. (If you already are programming 2 goals, now add a third.) Use the post-Alpha instructions to gain additional benefits from Alpha programming.

After using the post-Alpha instructions, come out of the Alpha dimension by the 1 to 5 method.

DAY 24 • EXERCISE 1

"NEEDS AND PURPOSES"

FUNDAMENTAL FACT OF LIFE

We all have subjective needs. These needs come from our positive and negative life experiences and they guide our conscious thoughts and actions.

Having established your goals, you must learn to communicate them to others. It is not enough to just ask someone to help you achieve a goal. Their understanding of your needs and purposes and the importance you attach to them will encourage others to help you.

Conversely, you must actively acquire data on other people's needs. If you wish to increase your affinity with people, you must increase your communication with them and find out what their needs are.

The more you understand another person's reality, the better you will be able to communicate with them. Plan, over a period of time, to spend at least 30 minutes with each person you consider important in your life, asking them what their needs are and sharing with them your needs. Make appointments today for this purpose.

If you are married to someone you are really crazy about but find their lovemaking technique unpleasant, then it is vital to your marriage to take time to exchange views on lovemaking. If you like to make love lying down and your partner likes to make love standing up, an exchange of views might lead to another method for mutual pleasure. If you don't communicate your needs you'll end up with bad sex and flat feet.

DAY 24 ● EXERCISE 2

"SELF ANALYSIS"

DEPROGRAMMING

Can you remember when:

You found your size didn't matter.

Someone thought you were skillful.

You were glad you had been slow in doing something.

You put a puzzle together.

You were glad you came early.

You won a struggle.

You made an unfriendly person submit to your will.

You succeeded in spite of others.

Someone's presence was reassuring to you.

You handled a difficult situation with someone well.

Your search was rewarded.

You found you had taken someone too seriously.

Your anxiety was unnecessary.

Your tears were followed by relief.

DAY 24 ● EXERCISE 3

"IMAGINATIVE EVOCATION OF OTHER SENSATIONS"

MIND DEVELOPMENT

Imagine the following smells:

A broiled steak.

An onion.

A rose.

A lilac.

The ocean.

A zoo.

The smell of the person you love best.

Smoke.

Chinese food.

Italian food.

A hospital.

A new car.

A new leather jacket.

A musty apartment.

A baby with a dirty diaper.

Gasoline.

Spices.

DAY 24 ● EXERCISE 4

GOAL 1 & 2

PROGRAMMING

Enter the Alpha dimension by the 5 to 1 method, the body relaxation method, and the 10 to 1 method. Program your first goals.

After programming your first goal for 10 minutes, introduce a second goal and program that for approximately five to ten minutes. (If you already are programming 2 goals, now add a third.) Use the post-Alpha instructions to gain additional benefits from Alpha programming.

After using the post-Alpha instructions, come out of the Alpha dimension by the 1 to 5 method.

DAY 25 ● EXERCISE 1

"ACKNOWLEDGE-
MENT & VALIDATION"
FUNDAMENTAL FACT OF LIFE

As we have mentioned earlier, all of us suffer to some extent from intimacy avoidance. Most of us have failed to receive all the love that we sought and so we seek other forms of emotional gratification. One form of positive emotional gratification is acknowledgement.

Acknowledgement may be defined as letting someone know that you received their message. In essence you tell that person, "I know that you are here and I acknowledge your existence."

You probably had the experience of a friend not responding to a cheerful hello from you. The friend did not acknowledge your existence. We all repeatedly put forth considerations to other people and constantly find that many of these considerations are invalidated. For instance, you may say to someone, "Isn't it wonderful that the war is over." Their response might be, "No, now there will be less money in the economy and I will be able to buy less." Your statement has thus been rejected or invalidated.

You must learn to choose the kind of person whose behavior you wish to validate. If you choose to validate someone's consideration you then share a common reality with that person and they therefore feel closer to you and can communicate with you better.

It is easier to validate someone's considerations if you can determine from the beginning that you are sympathetic to that person. You might find it hard to validate Hitler's opinions; an ardent Democrat's opinions when you are a staunch Republican; or the considerations of someone who thinks he is Napoleon.

If you choose to invalidate a person's statement you will reduce the common ground you share and also the bond of communication between you.

This is not to say that you should placate others. However, be certain to validate considerations when you can and carefully consider the consequences of invalidation which is a break in affinity, reality, and communication with others.

DAY 25 ● EXERCISE 2

"SELF ANALYSIS"

DEPROGRAMMING

Can you remember when:

Someone had to respect your right of ownership.

Something you thought was rare turned out to be ordinary.

You regained your energy.

You made a dog wag his tail.

You really earned the wages you were paid.

You took a walk with someone you liked.

You backed an unfriendly person against a wall.

You discovered you were strong.

You made an unfriendly person cry.

You were happy to see someone leave.

You were complimented on something you wrote.

You made somebody yell.

Somebody accepted an object you gave them.

Someone admired something you had.

You discovered you liked something you thought you disliked.

DAY 25 • EXERCISE 3

"IMAGINATIVE EVOCATION OF OTHER SENSATIONS"

MIND DEVELOPMENT

Refer to Day 24, Exercise 3, and repeat the exercise.

Imagine the following smells:

A broiled steak.

An onion.

A rose.

A lilac.

The ocean.

A zoo.

The smell of the person you love best.

Smoke.

Chinese food.

Italian food.

A hospital.

A new car.

A new leather jacket.

A musty apartment.

A baby with a dirty diaper.

Gasoline.

Spices.

DAY 25 • EXERCISE 4

GOAL 1 & 2

PROGRAMMING

Enter the Alpha dimension by the 5 to 1 method, the body relaxation method, and the 10 to 1 method. Program your first goals.

After programming your first goal for 10 minutes, introduce a second goal and program that for approximately five to ten minutes. (If you already are programming 2 goals, now add a third.) Use the post-Alpha instructions to gain additional benefits from Alpha programming.

After using the post-Alpha instructions, come out of the Alpha dimension by the 1 to 5 method.

DAY 26 ● EXERCISE 1

"THE STABLE DATUM CONCEPT"

FUNDAMENTAL FACT OF LIFE

Certain attitudes that we have and certain people with whom we interact are so basic to our existence, that we call these attitudes and people Stable Datum.

A Stable Datum is a basic fact, person, or object that we believe to be essential to our survival.

One hundred and fifty years ago, slavery was a stable datum in the South. Plantation owners considered slavery to be necessary to their lives. When Lincoln freed the slaves, he abolished the stable datum. When stable datum is upset, dynamic change and emotional upset always follow.

Wives and husbands are stable datums. They are people you rely upon in almost every aspect of your life. That is why a divorce may have such a shattering effect upon someone.

Related to the stable datum concept is the concept of Ally Loss. An ally is a stable datum. An ally is a person or pet upon whom one depends for his survival. The death of a mother, father, brother, other relative, friend or even a pet turtle triggers the survival mechanism and generates unconscious, automatic behavior.

You must learn to recognize the stable data in your life. You must prepare for the consequences when a Stable Datum withdraws and learn not to be overly attached to any particular Stable Datum. You can love that person or object but not be dependent on his or its existence. Always remember that people are not possessions.

You must also learn the effect that loss of an ally or a Stable Datum will have on someone else and understand the consequences in order to better deal with the emotional behavior that will follow.

DAY 26 ● EXERCISE 2

"RESTIMULATOR
LOG"

DEPROGRAMMING

Keep a small 3x5 spiral-bound notebook in your pocket and make notes about what restimulators cause uptight and unhappy behavior in your life. See which experiences or stimuli trigger survival-related experiences and generate inappropriate tense or fearful behavior. For instance, does bad weather, being kept waiting, or being rejected restimulate you and make you "uptight"?

List the date, time, stimuli, and behavior generated. The more detached you can be from yourself, the more you can be present to your behavior and note the restimulators that cause your unhappiness.

Ask yourself what earlier similar experiences have triggered behavior similar to what you have noted. Search your mind for those experiences so that you may begin to remove the burden you placed on yourself by these restimulators.

DAY 26 ● EXERCISE 3

"DEEP BREATHING"

MIND DEVELOPMENT

The purpose of this exercise if to bring you more in touch with your superconscious energy and to teach you to relax and take control of your body.

Place yourself in a completely relaxed position, remove all tight clothing and be sure that you are in a place that is free from interruption.

Take a deep breath and hold it to the count of 4. Now exhale. Do this four times.

Now place your right index finger in front of your right nostril taking a deep breath through your left nostril. Hold it for the count of 4. Now exhale. Repeat four times.

Now place your left index finger in front of your left nostril taking a deep breath through your right nostril. Hold it for the count of 4. Now exhale. Repeat four times.

Allow your entire body to completely relax, repeating this technique 10 times. As you get more proficient in deep breathing, you will experience a rush of insights and mental images which will help you achieve your goals.

Deep Breathing
Exercises

INHALE

EXHALE

DAY 26 ● EXERCISE 4

GOAL 1 & 2
PROGRAMMING

Enter the Alpha dimension by the 5 to 1 method, the body relaxation method, and the 10 to 1 method. Program your first goals.

After programming your first goal for 10 minutes, introduce a second goal and program that for approximately five to ten minutes. (If you already are programming 2 goals, now add a third.) Use the post-Alpha instructions to gain additional benefits from Alpha programming.

After using the post-Alpha instructions, come out of the Alpha dimension by the 1 to 5 method.

INHALE   EXHALE

DAY 27 • EXERCISE 1

"THE GAMES PEOPLE PLAY"

FUNDAMENTAL FACT OF LIFE

In practicing intimacy avoidance, people have learned to play games with each other as they seek substitute gratification for love.

People play the "See what you made me do game." If a person is feeling unsociable, he becomes engrossed in some activity which isolates him from people. If his wife or one of his children comes in looking for love and asks, "Where did you put the newspaper?" the interruption "causes" his pen to slip or paintbrush to drip or typewriter to miscue, whereupon he turns to the intruder and yells, "See what you made me do?" Of course, it is not the intruder that has caused this anger. It is the person himself who is only too happy to have an interruption since it gives him an opportunity to reject his wife or child. This game allows him to continue his pattern of intimacy avoidance. As a prize he has won a life of isolation.

Then, there is the "If I only could" game. Linda is with her friend Joanne. Linda says: "If only I was more attractive I could find a man to love." Joanne says: "Why don't I help you style your hair?" Linda says: "I don't have enough time now." Joanne says: "Why don't you go to the beauty parlor?" Linda says: "I don't earn enough money to be able to go to the beauty parlor." Joanne says: "Why not get a better job?" Linda says: "I am not attractive enough to get a better job." Joanne, exasperated after this exercise, gives up and thereby validates Linda's position that she is right to withdraw from intimate relationships.

By failing to continue this discussion, Joanne has validated Linda's consideration that she cannot find a man to love. Linda has skillfully played the "If-I-only-could" game and now as her prize she has won a life without love.

There is also the game called "Please don't kick me." Mr. X has a pathetic look on his face. He wears threadbare clothing and, meek and nervous, goes for a job interview. His voice cracks and he gives a nervous laugh. The interviewer looks at this person who is projecting "loser" signals and gives him exactly what he is seeking. He rejects him for the job and validates for Mr. X the idea that he cannot have a close business relationship or achieve personal success. Mr. X has put a sign on himself saying, "Please don't kick me," and therefore has tempted everyone into kicking him. His prize is a life of mediocrity and limitation.

Examine your relationships with others to see which games you are playing to avoid love and closeness. Examine others and the games they play.

But more importantly, reach out and love other people and reject the pattern of intimacy avoidance. Rid yourself of a life that is dominated by the hurts and hostilities of the past.

DAY 27 • EXERCISE 2

"EMOTIONAL OVERLOAD"

DEPROGRAMMING

An emotional overload is achieved by isolating yourself in a room free from any interrupting stimuli. You may not have any books to read. You may, however, have a pen and paper, if you wish to write anything down.

The room should be as spartan as possible, preferably only a bed and a straight chair. Isolate yourself in this room, free from any interruption and then systematically begin to eliminate all those defenses you use to block your mind from fully experiencing life or early painful experiences. Nail biting, face rubbing, masturbation and any diversionary efforts should not be permitted. Lie, sit, or stand, but systematically collapse all the erected barriers between you and being here now.

Smoking is not permitted and eating is not permitted, except at the end of a 12-hour cycle. No drugs or alcohol are permitted beginning 48 hours before you start the emotional overload exercise. Also, do not wear any clothing during the exercise.

Let whatever thoughts come into your mind surface. Sink into any feelings you have and allow yourself to fully experience those feelings. Allow your emotions to swell up and overload you with strong feelings.

DAY 27 • EXERCISE 3

"DEEP BREATHING"

MIND DEVELOPMENT

The purpose of this exercise if to bring you more in touch with your superconscious energy and to teach you to relax and take control of your body. This exercise is repeated from Day 26, Exercise 3.

Place yourself in a completely relaxed position, remove all tight clothing and be sure that you are in a place that is free from interruption.

Take a deep breath and hold it to the count of 4. Now exhale. Do this four times.

Now place your right index finger in front of your right nostril taking a deep breath through your left nostril. Hold it for the count of 4. Now exhale. Repeat four times.

Now place your left index finger in front of your left nostril taking a deep breath through your right nostril. Hold it for the count of 4. Now exhale. Repeat four times.

Allow your entire body to completely relax, repeating this technique 10 times. As you get more proficient in deep breathing, you will experience a rush of insights and mental images which will help you achieve your goals.

DAY 27 • EXERCISE 4

GOAL 1 & 2
PROGRAMMING

Enter the Alpha dimension by the 5 to 1 method, the body relaxation method, and the 10 to 1 method. Program your first goals.

After programming your first goal for 10 minutes, introduce a second goal and program that for approximately five to ten minutes. (If you already are programming 2 goals, now add a third.) Use the post-Alpha instructions to gain additional benefits from Alpha programming.

After using the post-Alpha instructions, come out of the Alpha dimension by the 1 to 5 method.

DAY 28 ● EXERCISE 1

"THE PYGMALION PRINCIPLE"

FUNDAMENTAL FACT OF LIFE

The Pygmalion Principle says: What you expect, is what you get. Your expectations guide your subconscious mind in its decision-making process and programs it with the behavior you have projected.

If you begin a love affair thinking in advance that all men are deceitful, you will find ways to validate your own consideration and have your lover deceive you. If you enter a business career with the expectation that all executives are dishonest, you will find ways to associate yourself with dishonest executives and validate your opinion.

And, if in fact your lover is not deceitful and the executive is not dishonest, you will make sure you accept only those bits of data into your consciousness that validate your decision. You will also choose to reject data which invalidate your decisions.

You can make the Pygmalion Principle work for you by recognizing that the mere act of expectancy is sufficient to influence the outcome of events in your life. To achieve a positive outcome, expect a positive outcome.

DAY 28   EXERCISE 2

"REDUCING CONDITIONED REFLEXES"

DEPROGRAMMING

Each of us has been conditioned during our lifetimes to respond to particular stimuli. This conditioning process may be caused by survival-related incidents or by the reinforcement of life experiences which create our attitudes and our behavior.

There is an exercise that helps you consciously negate a conditioned reflex pattern by refusing to respond to the stimuli with a standard response.

The following are examples of ways in which you can alter the pattern of response to stimuli:

1. When the telephone rings the next time, let it ring. Do not respond to it.

2. After you wash your hands leave the faucet running.

3. When sitting down at the dinner table, do not put a napkin on your lap.

4. Before going to sleep, do not turn the television set off. Let it run all night.

5. For the men, do not wear a tie to work. For the women, when you go shopping, dress in a fashion different from the one you ordinarily would when you go shopping, e.g., if you wear pantsuits, wear dungarees. If you wear dungarees, wear a skirt, etc.

DAY 28 EXERCISE 2 (con't.)

6. If you normally eat a large breakfast, eat a small one.

7. Go to a restaurant and if you generally leave a 10% tip, leave a 20% tip. If you generally leave a 20% tip, leave no tip at all.

8. Do not brush your teeth before you go to bed.

9. Whatever you customarily drink with your meal, drink something else, e.g., if you drink coffee, drink tea.

10. When someone says: Good morning, good afternoon, good evening or hello to you, use a different phrase in greeting them. If you usually say "Hello," say "Hi." If you say "Hi," say "Good evening." If you say "Good evening," say "How are you?" Constantly change your response to their greeting.

Now examine your behavior and begin to eliminate your own conditioned reflexes. Make a list of 10 conditioned reflex patterns you will try to change.

By consciously altering your stimuli response pattern, you begin to take control of your life. You will break stimulus response patterns which in turn will help you in terminating other, more important, stimulus response patterns.

DAY 28 ● EXERCISE 3

"THE EXERCISE
OF DICTIONARY
LOOK-UP"

MIND DEVELOPMENT

This exercise will enable you to experience the real meaning of words instead of the meaning you have hypnotized yourself into believing.

Open the dictionary and read ten definitions three times. Then spend at least two minutes thinking about the exact meaning of each word.

You will be amazed to find that you did not really understand the meaning of many words. This technique will increase your understanding of words and your ability to communicate.

For example read the definitions for love, loyalty, frustration, friend, won, achieve, happiness, sadness, experience, growth.

DAY 28 ● EXERCISE 4

GOAL 1 & 2
PROGRAMMING

Enter the Alpha dimension by the 5 to 1 method, the body relaxation method, and the 10 to 1 method. Program your first goals.

After programming your first goal for 10 minutes, introduce a second goal and program that for approximately five to ten minutes. (If you already are programming 2 goals, now add a third.) Use the post-Alpha instructions to gain additional benefits from Alpha programming.

After using the post-Alpha instructions, come out of the Alpha dimension by the 1 to 5 method.

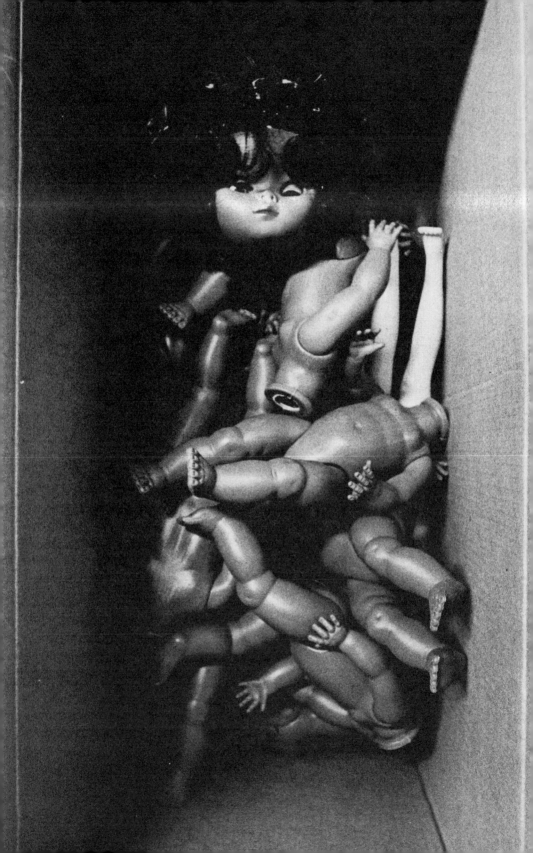

CHAPTER

7

DAY 29 — DAY 30

So long as little children are allowed to suffer, there is no true love in this world.

ISADORA DUNCAN

DAY 29 ● EXERCISE 1

"THE
MALFOPAH
THEORY"

FUNDAMENTAL FACT OF LIFE

Every person, to achieve success in life must have specific goals.

There is a mnemonic device call MALFOPAH. It is a list of eight goal categories which have worked well for many people.

"M" is for Mind related goals. (Ways to develop your mind).

"A" is for Appearance goals. (Ways to become more attractive).

"L" is for Love goals.

"F" is for Financial goals.

"O" is for Other people in your goals, (ways of helping them).

"P" is for Pleasure goals.

"A" is for Ability goals.

"H" is for Health goals.

You can examine your entire life and decide what you wish to do within each of these categories.

To use this exercise properly, get a large piece of paper or cardboard a few feet in length. Allow lots of space for each of the eight columns and begin to ask yourself what goals you have or should have in each of these eight categories.

First you may find only a few goals, if any, in each category. You may then have a sudden burst of insight and find six goals that you always wanted to achieve.

After you have established your goals, ask yourself, "What specialized knowledge do I need to achieve these goals?" For instance, if you are unhappy with your appearance ask yourself, "What do I need to learn about personal grooming, current fashions, hairstyles, cosmetic dentistry?" You can pursue your goal through the application of specialized knowledge and the creation of a detailed plan.

Review your goals once a week. Life is not stagnant and your goals should not be either. Devote about 10 minutes to goal review and goal adjustment in one of your Psycho-Calisthenics® sessions each week. Carefully measure the success you have achieved.

DAY 29 • EXERCISE 2

"AUTOBIOGRAPHY"

DEPROGRAMMING

An autobiography is a very effective tool to bring you into contact with experiences that are below the level of your consciousness.

Write your autobiography in quiet surroundings where you can concentrate.

Your life may be divided into the following chapters:

1. Experiences prior to school.

2. Experiences in elementary school.

3. Experiences in junior and senior high school.

4. Experiences in college and graduate school.

5. Work experiences prior to marriage.

6. Marriage experiences.

7. Experiences with your children.

8. Additional adult experiences (divorce, separation, living alone and so forth).

The above is merely a guideline and is not intended as a rigid format. It is the concept that is important.

Once you have completed the basic outline, begin to examine the most significant experiences in each classification. Be sure to allow yourself to be completely relaxed.

It might be helpful to enter the Alpha dimension. Outline the basic experiences for each classification, then proceed with another activity. Come back to the list of basic experiences, read them again and add any additional experiences which come to mind. Follow the same procedure a third time.

Now begin to write your autobiography, section by section. Start with the earliest experiences and work your way up to the present. Allow two lines of space after each line of writing so you can fill in additional experiences as you recall them.

After you have completed each section, go back and reread it so that you can supplement your autobiography.

When the autobiography is completed, ask yourself certain questions. Do not read the questions on the next page until you complete your autobiography so that they do not affect your writing.

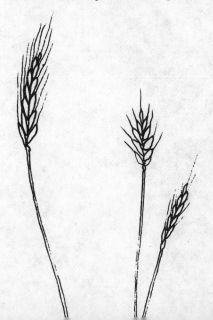

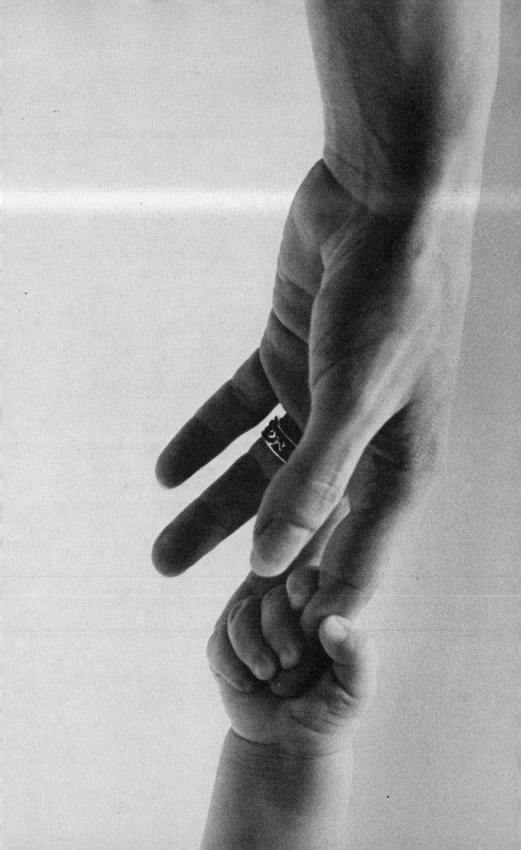

DAY 29 • EXERCISE 3

"THE DEVELOPMENT OF THE WILL"

MIND DEVELOPMENT

One of the principal goals of Psychosynthesis and Psycho-Calisthenics® is the development of the will. Will is the desire to achieve a goal.

1. As we are dealing with will in the conscious mind, it is essential to have a purpose because without a conscious aim the will cannot be developed. Once you know your purpose you must generate the will and the motivation to achieve it. Motivation always implies a set of values. We all have a scale of values but it may not be fully developed.

2. After developing a set of values, the second step is to deliberate. The goal must be important to you and it must also be attainable within your present ability.

3. The third stage of the development of the will is decision. Making a decision means that you must recognize that you cannot realistically have all options but must choose among reasonable alternatives.

The difficulty in making a decision is realizing that it involves your taking responsibility for that decision.

DAY 29 EXERCISE 3 (con't.)

4. The fourth stage of will is affirmation. Affirmation involves faith, which is a firm conviction that something can be done. It is related to the Pygmalion Principle that what you expect is what you get. If conviction is lacking, real affirmation cannot be made.

Affirmation is a declaration to oneself. The intensity of the affirmation determines the extent of its effectiveness.

5. The fifth stage is planning. It means organizing your activities according to a clearly outlined program. To do this you need a complete understanding of the various stages that have to be realized from the beginning of your efforts to the achievement of the ultimate goal.

Develop your will as it relates to an important goal you would like to achieve by following the 5 stages of development.

6. The Sixth stage is the direction or execution. Two things are required for will development: driving energy and persistence.

Now that you understand the concept of will you can begin to exercise it.

A. Mobilize your energy. Enter the alpha dimension. Picture to yourself as vividly as possible all the unfortunate consequences to yourself and to others which have actually occurred and those which might occur in the future as a result of your limited will. Study each carefully and then when you leave the alpha dimension make a list of them. Allow the feelings which these recollections and forecasts arise in you to affect you intensly. Feel the shame and dissatisfaction with yourself at having shrunk from the responsibility and the urgent desire to change things.

B. Picture to yourself as vividly as possible all the advantages which the training of your will can being to you. Visualize all the benefits and satisfaction which you and others can have. Examine them carefully and write them down when you leave the alpha dimension. Allow the feelings aroused by these thoughts to culminate in an intense desire to realize your potential and the strong impulse to begin at once.

C. Imagine yourself having a strong, persistent will. Focus your attention on your efforts, your persistence and your total self-control. See yourself successfully attaining your goals. Think of situations similar to ones in which you have previously failed and see yourself acting successfully with a strong will.

D. Find reading material that will help you expand and reinforce determination of your will. Read books in which the main character successfully achieves his goals.

E. Learn to perform exercises merely for the sake of performing them. Decide that every morning at 7:30 you will do ten push-ups. Train yourself to have persistence and consistency. Learn to retire at a fixed hour every night for a week, resolutely interrupting anything to follow your schedule.

Be aware of your own behavior and observe yourself as you begin to develop and exercise your will. Note your success and failures. The more you develop your will, the more you will achieve your purpose.

DAY 29 • EXERCISE 4

PROGRAMMING

As you begin to develop your repertoire of programming techniques to achieve long and short term goals through the use of Psycho-Calisthenics, think about a series of positive statements that are essential to the body-mind oneness.

Try to include the following positive statements and thoughts for better, more successful living, in your daily programming. The daily and continuous use of this extremely important positive input is like the daily basic routine of the professional musician or athlete who is constantly sharpening his skills and techniques.

Try the following:

1. The statements should be programmed after your goals, just before leaving the Alpha dimension by the 1 to 5 method.

2. Memorize two additional statements each day until they are all internalized.

3. Regardless of the level of the Alpha dimension you use, begin immediately. When you are traveling from place to place, enter the Alpha dimension by the 5 to 1 method and reinforce your programming. Even at lunch, take an Alpha break. You can tape these sessions and play them back while driving. The input will be valuable and effective.

POSITIVE STATEMENTS AND THOUGHTS FOR BETTER, MORE SUCCESSFUL LIVING

1. Every day I am developing and using my mind for creative and constructive purposes.

2. Every day, in every way, I am getting better and better, healthier and healthier, happier and happier.

3. I am developing and increasing my mental capabilities needed to help myself and others.

4. Every day I will keep my thoughts positive and loving. I will become all that it is possible for me to become.

5. Every day I am learning to develop greater awareness and understanding of myself and others.

6. I will always have complete control of all my faculties and senses at all levels of consciousness.

7. Positive benefits will come to me every day through positive thoughts.

8. I want to respond only to positive thoughts and actions.

9. Life is here. Life is now. I am life. I celebrate and love it.

POSITIVE STATEMENTS AND THOUGHTS FOR HEALTHIER LIVING

1. I will always maintain a healthy body and mind completely free of organic or psychosomatic disorders.

2. I will always strive to give my body the proper food, rest and exercise it requires for perfect health.

3. Every system, every muscle, every gland, and every cell in my body will always function in a completely harmonious, healthy manner.

4. I will always strive to have perfect health. My mind knows it and my body shows it.

DAY 30 • EXERCISE 1

"THE CRISIS CONCEPT"

FUNDAMENTAL FACT OF LIFE

As you begin your voyage to greater happiness and purpose in life, the seas will not always be calm. Suddenly things you believed to be so are not so. Many of the things you held as Stable Data are in fact not stable. Your perception of others will motivate you to change allies. The career that you have always believed was essential to you may no longer be essential. The marital partner you considered a necessary and loving part of your life may now be neither necessary nor loving.

You suddenly find your survival threatened because in fact you are no longer the same person you were before. You are changing and growing. You are experiencing hurt on a conscious level and living life to its fullest.

You are having soul-shattering insights. You are no longer a robot. You have feelings. You love and hate. You have greater awareness. You are aware that your environment is made up of limitless opportunities. Artificial barriers begin to crumble and you take chances. You win and lose, but you live. As you read this book some of the fundamental facts of life have begun to make an impact on your knowledge of yourself. It is therefore natural that you may become a bit fearful. You are going through a crisis and may feel as if you are losing your mind.

A crisis is a turning point in your life for better or worse. This feeling is normal and is experienced by all people whose consciousness is expanding.

As you continue to practice Psycho-Calisthenics® there will be fewer lows and more highs. Your personal growth is not a threat to your survival, but a survival support system. You will hang breathlessly on the Moment of Now.

DAY 30 ● EXERCISE 2

"QUESTIONS FOR YOUR AUTOBIOGRAPHY"
DEPROGRAMMING

ASK YOURSELF THE FOLLOWING QUESTIONS:

1. What were the twelve most significant experiences in my life?

2. What early experiences in my life were significant in shaping my behavior?

3. What were the twelve best things I have done in my life?

4. What were the twelve worst things I have done in my life?

5. What twelve people have been most significant in shaping my attitudes and behavior?

6. What was the happiest time of my life and why was it happier than others?

7. What was the saddest time of my life and why was it sadder than others?

8. What are the most significant things that I have learned about myself from this autobiography?

9. In reviewing my autobiography what would I like to change about myself?

10. How can I plan my future so that I am in control of my life and what do I want for my future?

Write the answers to each of these questions as fully as possible. Reflect on the questions and on the answers. Be aware of your past behavior without judging or criticizing yourself. Try to learn from the past so that you can make use of the present.

DAY 30 ● EXERCISE 3

THE DEVELOPMENT OF THE WILL

MIND DEVELOPMENT

Refer to Day 29, Exercise 3 and repeat the entire exercise.

One of the principal goals of psychosynthesis and Psycho-Calisthenics is the development of the will. Will is the desire to achieve a goal.

A. Mobilize your energy. Enter the alpha dimension. Picture to yourself as vividly as possible all the unfortunate consequences to yourself and to others which have actually occurred and those which might occur in the future as a result of your limited will. Study each carefully and then when you leave the alpha dimension make a list of them. Allow the feelings which these recollections and forecasts arise in you to affect you intensely. Feel the shame and dissatisfaction with yourself at having shrunk from the responsibility and the urgent desire to change things.

B. Picture to yourself as vividly as possible all the advantages which the training of your will can being to you. Visualize all the benefits and satisfaction which you and others can have. Examine them carefully and write them down when you leave the alpha dimension. Allow the feelings aroused by these thoughts to culminate in an intense desire to realize your potential and the strong impulse to begin at once.

C. Imagine yourself having a strong, persistent will. Focus your attention on your efforts, your persistence and your total self-control. See yourself successfully attaining your goals. Think of situations similar to ones in which you have previously failed and see yourself acting successfully with a strong will.

D. Find reading material that will help you expand and reinforce determination of your will. Read books in which the main character successfully achieves his goals.

E. Learn to perform exercises merely for the sake of performing them. Decide that every morning at 7:30 you will do ten push-ups. Train yourself to have persistence and consistency. Learn to retire at a fixed hour every night for a week, resolutely interrupting anything to follow your schedule.

Be aware of your own behavior and observe yourself as you begin to develop and exercise your will. Note your success and failures. The more you develop your will, the more you will achieve your purpose.

DAY 30 ● EXERCISE 4

GOAL 1 & 2

PROGRAMMING

Reread and repeat Day 29, Exercise 4.

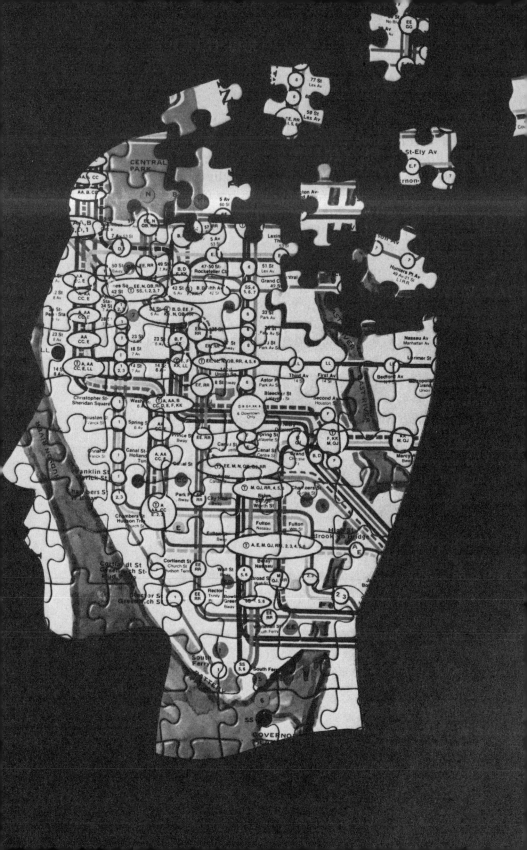

CONCLUSION

Life is out there. It is yours for the taking. This book provides a workable plan involving the best of dozens of the most important and successful mental disciplines. You can now decide whether to think of this as just an interesting book, as a way to acquire some knowledge that you can adapt to your own behavior, or as a start of a new life. You can make substantial use of this book and build your own Psycho-Calisthenics® program with exercises that really help you achieve your goals in life.

You can take complete Psycho-Calisthenics® week-end or cassette courses and learn more exercises. But Psycho-Calisthenics® is not a religion or a dogma. I do not seek disciples. I am only a guide, not a guru. I respect and honor you as an emerging spiritual being. The rest is up to you.

I wish you love and fulfillment in life and I would like to meet you now or in the future, in this dimension or another, for we are all together on the journey to Love and Happiness.

Love

Steven

☐ I am interested in taking the Psycho-Calisthenics® 30 hour weekend course. I understand that the fee for this course is $150. and that there may be a waiting list. Many additional exercises not covered in the book are discussed in the course.

☐ I am interested in taking the Psyco-Calisthenic® cassette learning course. I understand that this course is done at home at my own pace and with casette tapes, written charts, lectures and related materials. A free question and answer correspondence service is also included with the cassette program. I understand that the fee for this course is $125. and that my success in this course depends upon my own efforts. There are a large number of additional exercises not included in the book.

☐ I am interested in becoming a distributor consultant for Psycho-Calisthenics® in my area. I recognize that my interest in Human Potential is more significant than the investment requirements which will vary by area size.

Please contact me so that we can arrange and review the necessary details:

NAME. . . . .

ADDRESS . . . .

CITY & STATE . . . .

TELEPHONE NUMBER . . . .

BEST TIME TO CALL . . . .

TO DETACH, CUT ON DOTTED LINE.

· ·

· · · · · · · · FOLD ALONG THIS LINE, SEAL, STAMP AND MAIL ·

PLACE
STAMP
HERE

BUSINESS REPLY CARD

PSYCHO-CALISTHENICS
112 CENTRAL PARK SOUTH
Suite 11F
New York City, N.Y. 10019